ENGAGING
A NEW GENERATION

A Vision for Reaching Catholic Teens

Frank Mercadante

Our Sunday Visitor Publishing Division
Our Sunday Visitor, Inc.
Huntington, IN 46750

Nihil Obstat:
Msgr. Michael Heintz, Ph.D.
Censor Librorum

Imprimatur:
✠ Kevin C. Rhoades
Bishop of Fort Wayne-South Bend
March 19, 2012

The *Nihil Obstat* and *Imprimatur* are declarations that a work is free from doctrinal or moral error. It is not implied that those who have granted the *Nihil Obstat* and *Imprimatur* agree with the contents, opinions, or statements expressed.

ISBN: 978-1-59276-722-9 (Inventory No. T1043)
eISBN: 978-1-61278-222-5
LCCN: 2012934466

Interior design by M. Urgo
Cover design by Lindsey Riesen
Cover photo by Veer

PRINTED IN THE UNITED STATES OF AMERICA

Endorsements

This text fills a great need. Anyone working with youth will want to read it. You will better understand the religious and spiritual lives of the young and how to engage them as disciples of Jesus. It provides a wealth of ways to reach the young.

Bishop Gerald F. Kicanas, Bishop of Tucson

In *Engaging a New Generation*, Frank Mercadante masterfully and succinctly outlines some of the big shifts that have taken place within culture and the Church. He's captured some of the changes that are present in the lives and customs of contemporary teens and how we, as Catholic communities, need to re-frame our efforts to minister to them. Frank provides a great service here ... he names current realities we feel and see with precision and then offers insights and directions to help those who desire to serve, love and bring young people to Christ.

This book doesn't shy away from challenges; on the contrary, Frank is faithfully prophetic. He offers pointed, solid advice filled with hope as he lays out what parents, teachers, coaches, ministers, and other adults can do to support and engage young people with a vibrant, living faith. A superb reflection and powerful overview of the contemporary context and challenges of Catholic youth ministry.

Mike Patin, international Catholic speaker and "faith horticulturist"

Whoever wants the next generation of Catholic youth the most will get them. It is not enough just to entertain them; that is a failed model of the past. We need to engage them in a conversation and experience of the genius of Catholicism. Let Frank Mercadante show you how!

Matthew Kelly, *New York Times* best-selling author of *Rediscover Catholicism* and founder of Dynamiccatholic.com

As I read Frank's book, the words of Jesus continually rang in my mind: "No one pours new wine into old wineskins." Yet we as a Church often hope to reach today's young people with yesterday's approach — and then wonder why they don't respond. Frank Mercadante's excellent book, *Engaging a New Generation,* empowers adults with a new cultural perspective on youth culture and challenges those who work with the young Church to not just educate or entertain this new generation, but to *engage* them. This book is a must read for anyone who hopes to pass on the faith to teenagers today.

Bob Rice, speaker, author, musician, and Professor of Catechetics at Franciscan University of Steubenville

By expanding our vocabulary for what is right before our eyes, Frank Mercadante opens contemporary opportunities for youth ministry. We can look forward with more hope and joy. By knowing why certain plans work, we have a better chance to repeat them. *Engaging a New Generation* is as much about vibrant parish faith as it is about our young people.

Bishop Timothy Doherty, Diocese of Lafayette-in-Indiana

Frank Mercadante has used his vast experience in youth ministry to craft a modern manifesto for reaching young people today. We all know that teenagers have changed, and that we *must* do something different to reach them. This book gives the *why* and the *how*. It's a must-read for today's youth ministers, teachers, and catechists — even parents!

Jim Beckman, Director of Youth Evangelization and Leadership, Augustine Institute

Frank Mercadante's passion for the young Church and his commitment to a comprehensive approach to pastoral ministry is evident on every page of *Engaging a New Generation: A Vision for Reaching Catholic Teens*. His book provides an analysis of the "territory" for youth ministry, including an overview of the postmodern world, current research on the millennial generation, and a review of parish life. Frank then offers a ministry "map," a vision for effectively navigating that territory, and he provides concrete descriptions of a ministry structure that fosters effective ministry. Central to this work is Frank's concept of "immanuelizing," anchoring our understanding of evangelization in a ministerial approach that is experiential, incarnational, and communal. *Engaging a New Generation* is now on my list of "must-read" books on Catholic youth ministry.

Bob McCarty, D.Min., Executive Director, National Federation for Catholic Youth Ministry

This book comes from deep inside the field of youth ministry and is the work of a successful and reflective practitioner. It is theological, sociological, practical, pastoral, and scriptural. Frank gets the reader completely current and thoroughly up to date and then offers directions that have worked for him.

Dr. Mike Carotta, author, national consultant

Frank Mercadante is in it to win it for today's teens. *Engaging A New Generation* gives powerful insight into teens today and presents an emphasis on the need for relational ministry led by individuals who themselves are living authentic and on-fire Catholic lives.

Randy Raus, Life Teen President / CEO

The Catholic Church is being impacted by sharp cultural transformations that are negatively impacting ministry with young people. Frank Mercadante clearly identifies these cultural shifts and shares important current research on youth and families. He also proposes an incarnational approach to evangelizing youth and families that addresses these cultural shifts. This is an important contribution to re-visioning adolescent catechesis and Catholic youth ministry for the twenty-first century.

Jeffrey Kaster, Ed.D, Saint John's University
School of Theology and Seminary, Collegeville

This book is the most significant resource I have read, not only for youth ministry but for parish ministry, in the last ten years. If you want to know how the Church can respond to the youth of today, read this book.

Peter Denio, Standards for Excellence Coordinator,
The National Leadership Roundtable on Church Management

If you are looking for insight into *today's* young people, read this book! If you are looking for a twenty-first century vision of youth ministry, read this book! If you want to help young people develop a vibrant, life-transforming faith, read this book! Let Frank Mercadante be your guide to effective ministry with young people and teach you how to become a faith-filled matchmaker for young people!

John Roberto, LifelongFaith Associates

Dedication

I'd like to dedicate this book to my six Millennial Generation children, Sarah, Michael, Rebekah, Angela, Deborah, and Daniel. You have made me a much better man and minister to young people. You've taught me a theology of accompaniment (without knowing it). And, in many ways, this book represents our conversations. By listening to you, you've taught me more about engaging a new generation than you'll ever know.

Acknowledgments

Like any work, this book would not have been possible without the input, support, and encouragement of so many people. At the top of my list stands Bert Ghezzi. A modern-day Barnabus, Bert's ongoing encouragement has been a consistent source of strength. I only hope to be for others what he has been for me.

I am so grateful to the entire "Epapharus" team who so kindly and generously prayed for me during the writing of this book. I credit you for any good that may come from this work.

I want to thank the many supporters of Cultivation Ministries, whose generosity afforded me the time to write this book. I share with you any fruit that comes from this work.

I want to express my gratitude to Ed and Joan Kramer, who so graciously provided their Galena home for me to write. The peace, quiet, and beauty provided the perfect environment for reflection and writing.

I want to thank Jennifer Kuhn for her invaluable editing. Thanks for making me a better writer. I am also grateful to Woodeene Koenig-Bricker. You have made this a better book by your valuable insights, editing, and organization.

I also want to thank John Roberto for his many honest and helpful insights. I so appreciate your generosity. Additionally, I am grateful to Marc Cardaronella, Matt Decker, Vince Guider, Craig Gould, Michelle Kilbourne, and Sarah Mercadante for the valuable feedback.

Finally, I want to thank my wife, Diane. What a gift God gave me in you. Your companionship, partnership, and support over the last thirty years have been the greatest joy of my life.

Contents

Introduction

In the 2007 motion picture *The Invasion*, Nicole Kidman plays Carol Bennell, a Washington, D.C., psychiatrist who observes changes in the personality of a client, her ex-husband, and finally the general population. In the course of what appears to be a routine morning, Bennell is uneasy. She says, "Something is happening. I don't know what it is, but I can feel it." She then turns to her companion and asks, "Have you noticed anything?"

Let's ask the same question. Have you noticed anything different about twenty-first-century teens? Although the teens physically resemble adolescents of the past (excluding expansive ink and multiple piercings), do they seem to think and see life differently than those of just a few years ago? When it comes to church activities, does it seem like what was "tried and true" for teens no longer works?

If you are vaguely uneasy about youth ministry, you're onto something. Something has distinctly changed among twenty-first-century teens. We can't always name it or articulate it profoundly, but we can feel it.

My Youth Ministry Experience

Over the past thirty years I have been involved in full-time Catholic youth ministry. After a life-altering conversion experience in late high school, I could think of nothing better to invest my life in than sharing the same Jesus who so transformed my life with others. With Catholic youth ministry still in its infancy, I ended up at Wheaton College, an evangelical Protestant institution that boasted of a graduate named Billy Graham. Not only did I learn how to correctly pronounce the word "evangelism," I became passionate about practicing it with anyone who would listen and even with those who wouldn't. A godly and open-minded pastor who was not put off by my *evangelicalese* dialect hired me.

As a novice parish youth minister, I cut my ministerial teeth on Gen X teens, those born between the mid-sixties and very early eighties. In many ways, Gen Xers followed *The Field of Dreams* mandate, "If you build it, they will come." Over a ten-year period, we developed programs for almost every day of the week. The sweeping menu included a teen outreach center, weight room, monthly retreats, weekly discipleship groups, before-school peer ministry leadership training, large group evangelistic gatherings, outside ministry and service opportunities, travel to large youth conferences, and more.

We built it, and they came! There were years when twice the number of registered parish teens attended our events. Over time, teen involvement swelled to mega youth ministry status with over 500 high schoolers attending our events. Reversing roles, local Protestant pastors bemoaned the fact that their teens were migrating to a Catholic youth ministry. Numbers aside, many teens experienced deep conversion and the desire to follow Jesus as a disciple, going on to serve the church in professional ministerial roles in youth ministry, religious education, and priesthood.

Youth ministry was going so well that I felt compelled by the need of other local Catholic parishes and a sense of personal call to export my "success." Leaving my parish position, I founded Cultivation Ministries, a not-for-profit youth ministry organization that assisted parishes in developing or revitalizing their parish youth ministries. What began with a single individual and a local Chicago-based effort grew into a ten-person staff and national ministry within several years.

Our staff was very busy developing resources, building parish youth ministries, and producing large youth rallies and conferences.

Change in the Air

Something happened as we approached the new millennium. Building a dynamic, disciple-making Catholic youth ministry had never been child's play, but the difficulty factor suddenly seemed to be exponentially multiplied. Young people were not coming simply because we built it. It was easy for us church folk — almost a default chorus line — to blame the ever-expanding school programs, zealous coaches, and complacent parents for a decline in our attendance. But it was only a smoke screen that camouflaged a deeper reality. Beyond stylistic preferences, young people were thinking and seeing life differently. I was beginning to feel like a youth ministry newbie — like the last twenty years meant nothing in this new era.

"Every few hundred years in Western history there occurs a sharp transformation.... Within a few short decades, society rearranges itself — its worldview; its basic values; its social and political structure; its arts; its key institutions.... Fifty years later, there is a new world and the people born then cannot even imagine the world in which their grandparents lived and into which their own parents were born. We are currently living through just such a transformation."[1]

—Peter Drucker, *Post-Capitalist Society*

The following are just a few examples of common changes and shifts in teen perspectives.

From Formal Promotion to Personal Connection

Send out a flyer and Gen X teens were more than likely to make an appearance. For today's teens, however, conventional promotions (flyers, mailings, announcements, etc.) are almost subconsciously filtered into mental junk mail folders. With a deluge of information, advertising, and more opportunities than time, teens are more distrustful of impersonal invitations. They require a more intimate connection for an invitation to register on their radar screens. Besides, many never actually open their "snail mail." Furthermore, bulletin and Mass announcements are fairly ineffectual because teens are often MIA for Sunday liturgy or, if present, see the invitations as remote, institutional, formal, and impersonal. In the end, the result is a decline in interest and attendance.

From Inheriting Faith to Choosing Faith

Previous youth generations were more apt to inherit the faith of their families; faith was generally passed down. In the past, we hedged our bets on wayward Catholic youth and young adults eventually returning to the faith of their childhood. While constructing their own faith convictions, values, and beliefs they would often bypass the Church, entertaining alternative life routes. More often than not, however, they returned to the Church in order to raise their children in the same faith tradition of their own childhood. Furthermore, there was a greater sense of institutional loyalty. Ironically, even Catholic parents who rarely attended Mass were fiercely loyal to the

Church. They often revealed their claws when one of their cubs ventured into the den of a differing faith tradition.

It's no longer a sure bet that young adults will return to their church of origin when getting married or raising children. The majority fails to return to any church and those who do go back often choose a different faith tradition.[2] Teens are not inheriting their faith as much as they are choosing their faith. In her research of adolescents and church, Carol Lytch concludes, "Passing on faith to the next generation is challenging today in a new way. In fact, 'passing on the faith' is no longer the task it used to be. Teens *choose* faith instead. American society has changed to favor individual choice of a highly personal religion that is less tethered to religious traditions and institutions."[3]

Past generations certainly had a choice. It was just limited. You chose church or you chose hell. Most chose church. Today, teens will not commit unless they find and experience meaning. Furthermore, today's young people are accustomed to choosing between gymnastics or dance, soccer or football, painting or theatre. Conditioned by a culture of choice, they are somewhat impervious to obligatory motivations and past forms of Catholic guilt. Possessing more options than hours, young people are *choosing* whether to be involved in church, and for reasons beyond family tradition or institutional loyalty. In a Google age, the Church is not the only spigot for the spiritually thirsty. But when today's teens are attracted to church, "they are attracted because the churches engage them in intense states of self-transcendence uniting emotional and cognitive processes. Churches 'catch' them on three hooks: a sense of belonging, a sense of meaning, and opportunities to develop competence."[4]

From Attractional to Authentic

Gen X teens enthusiastically responded to *evangetainment*. They were transfixed by emotionally moving drama, humorous talks, and reflective visual media. On the other hand, the emerging generation is impatient with stationary approaches and passive learning. They prefer engagement rather than entertainment. Twenty-first-century teens hunger for a more interactive and participatory experience.

While training novice youth ministers over the years, I would passionately proclaim, "The gospel is the greatest news the world has ever known and we must present it in a great way — with the dignity it deserves." For late Boomer and Gen X teens that meant slick, cool, and expensive productions that mirrored the quality of the larger culture. The less it reminded you of church (and the typically amateurish and archaic approaches) the more likely you drew a crowd. But the emerging teen population is dubious of the religious professionalism, preferring something more real, authentic, or *unplugged*. Presenting the gospel with the dignity it deserves means something entirely different to this generation.

My oldest son, Michael, a poster child for the emerging generation, gave me an education on their perspective towards "presenting the gospel with the dignity it deserves." When he was 18, a friend invited him to his baptism at a nearby evangelical Protestant, seeker-style mega church. Michael was happy to go in support of his friend. A large percentage of this church's membership was comprised of former Catholics. Knowing a number of my own peers who had left some of the local Catholic parishes for this church, I was curious how Michael would respond.

As he and another friend pulled into the driveway after the baptism, I made a beeline to the car. "So, what did you think?" I immediately asked.

"I hated it," he quickly interjected. His friend nodded in enthusiastic agreement. I'm not going to lie — I was shocked.

"What do you mean?" I inquired.

"Well, first of all, that place had the best of everything. You should have seen the sound system, projection screens, and comfortable seating. It was clear they took every penny collected and invested back into their own comfort and benefit. It's a 'country club' church. Shouldn't the church be about the poor? And, you should have seen the pastor. He wore a suit way too expensive for a man of the cloth. He talked more like a television talk show host than a pastor. He was just way too slick for me."

Astonished with his assessment, I could only mutter, "Huh." Michael's story went on — which brings us to another distinctive change in this emerging generation.

From Relationships as Strategies of Influence to Relationships for Relationship Sake

"The baptism was a farce," he went on. "After each person was dunked on stage, they shared their conversion story. I thought that would be cool. I like to hear people's faith stories. But they had a different agenda. By the second person, it became clear to me that their stories weren't so much about them as they were about us! We were invited to 'get saved' and be evangelized into their church. They weren't upfront with us. I felt duped."

Reading between the lines, Michael was articulating an important distinction for his generation: Relationships should not be used as a strategy for influence.[5]

For years, relational youth ministry was built on the mantra "earn the right to be heard."[6] Once we demonstrated interest in young people's lives by being relationally present, and built a sense of trust, they would become open to the gospel message. This approach worked with Boomer and Gen X teens, as they inquired, "Will you accept me for who I am?" However, a nuance in Millennial Generation teens' query is a complete game-changer. They ask, "Will you accept me for who I am *not*?" In other words, does the relationship stand on its own or does it exist for a hidden motive? Today's teens are suspicious and put off by relationships with an agenda. They hunger for relationships for relationship sake.

Today's youth are a different breed and youth ministry leaders are beginning to question our allegiance and use of older practices. Mark Oestreicher, the former president of Youth Specialties, one of the largest and most influential youth ministry organizations, wrote to thousands of youth ministers stating, "… many of our assumptions and practices in youth ministry are in need of major or minor overhaul."[7] Bob McCarty, the Executive Director for the National Federation for Catholic Youth Ministry (N.F.C.Y.M.), describes this moment by saying, "We are navigating new territories with old, outdated maps."[8]

The Crossroads

Catholic youth ministry stands at a crossroads. As we stand at the intersection, may we be reminded of Jesus' words, "For whoever wants to save his life will lose it, but whoever loses his life for me and for the gospel will save it" (Mark 8:35). Trying to go back to an earlier era and save the Church as we know it may mean losing a generation that doesn't relate any longer to our approaches and methodologies. In many ways we are presented with an incredible opportunity to become more real, loving, tolerant, community-oriented, and service-focused. Leonard Sweet poses the rhetorical questions "Will *we* live the time God has given *us*? Or will *we* live a time *we* would prefer to have?"[9]

FOR CONSIDERATION

- What is your experience of today's youth? What differences have you noticed in the way they relate to adults?
- Do you believe today's teens are choosing their faith, not inheriting it? If true, how does this change how we do church?
- Carol Lytch says we catch youth on the hooks of a sense of belonging, a sense of meaning, and opportunities to develop competence. How well does your parish catch young people on these hooks? In what ways can you make improvements?
- How can religious "professionals" become more real, authentic, and unplugged in a totally wired world?
- From your experience, how has relational youth ministry changed with today's teens?
- What parts of your youth ministry are working? What parts aren't working? What areas do you see need change?

Notes

1. Peter Drucker, *Post-Capitalist Society*, New York: Harper's Business, 1993. Page 1.
2. Martinson 2000; Barna 2001; Olson 2003.
3. Carol Lytch, *Choosing Church*. Louisville: Westminster John Knox Press, 2004. Page 13.
4. Carol Lytch, *Choosing Church*. Louisville: Westminster John Knox Press, 2004. Page 25.
5. In his book *Revisiting Relational Youth Ministry*, Andrew Root profoundly shifted the youth ministry community from commonly practicing relational ministry as "relationship as a means to a goal" to relationships as the goal.
6. A phrase originally coined by Jim Rayburn, the founder of the para-church youth ministry organization Young Life.
7. A letter sent by Youth Specialties around 2006.
8. Bob would frequently give presentations to youth ministry leaders with this title, describing some of these changes in the cultural landscape.
9. Leonard Sweet, *Post-Modern Pilgrims*. B & H Publishing Group, Nashville, 2000, page 47.

CHAPTER ONE

WE DON'T HAVE
A YOUTH PROBLEM ...

The ministerial challenges of adapting to a new world are not unique to the twenty-first century. Past spiritual innovators have had to negotiate the uncertainty of changing times. With the dawning of the modern era, St. John Bosco faced a similar, hazy crossroad. Grappling with a youth problem in newly industrialized Turin, John Bosco could have stood frozen in paralysis, defaulting to entrenched methodologies, and blaming a new generation for not responding to what has always worked in the past. Or, interpreting the present youth rebelliousness as an impending eschatological sign, he could have retreated to the safety of the saved, awaiting Jesus' return.

Instead, John Bosco chose to respond to the situation as an innovator. Troubled by the plight of neglected and unsupervised youth, he squarely faced its reality. He sought to reach out and save young teens from a life of crime and vice by building trusted relationships with them, embodying and teaching Jesus' love, and drawing them into communities of belonging. During an era of secularization and decline in supernatural belief, he drew young people to the faith with many signs and wonders. Although he left this earth in 1888, his example of ministerial innovation and resilience remains a standard for facing changing times. But before we begin to look at what we can do today in terms of innovation and resilience, we have to pause for a moment and define a few key terms.

Modernism and Postmodernism

We live in a postmodern world. Postmodernism turns on several key ideas that ultimately dispute the tenets of modernism. Therefore, it can be best understood when contrasted with modernism. The Enlightenment period gave birth to the modern mind, which thought that through the use of human intellect, employing rational and scientific thought, we could discover the laws that govern the universe and utilize them to make a better world. Modernism was optimistic, predicting increasing human progress and agreement as human reason would eventually lead us to unite on universal truths in science, government, economics, technology, etc. Once we found objective truth, it would bring about harmony, agreement, and the right way of seeing life. The concrete results were promising: industrial progress, medical advancement, technological breakthroughs, and the colonization of backward cultures. Modernism seemed to promise a bright utopian future for planet Earth.

The twentieth century, however, cast a dark shadow over this sunny outlook. The most "enlightened" cultures of Western Europe used their technological and bureaucratic progress to perfect the most efficient and effective methods of human slaughter and genocide. After two world wars, the threat of nuclear destruction, the Jewish Holocaust, industrial pollution and more, the world was not uniting in agreement and progressing in the most important arena of life: the service of humanity. Poverty, racial and ethnic discord, crime, and a host of other social problems continued to plague modern society.

Postmodernism emerged from the apparent failures of modernism. Postmodern thinkers challenged modern thought on several fronts. First, a postmodern perspective erodes the surety of human reason as the exclusive purveyor of truth. The claim that the mind can know objective truth, a truth that stands outside our world, is impossible. Everything observed occurs within history, context, and perspective. Furthermore, it is conveyed through language that is imprecise and subject to interpretation. Like the Emperor who had no clothes, the nakedness of the human intellect as the sole means to objective truth became obvious to postmodern philosophers.

The dethroning of rational thought opened the door to additional approaches for mining truth. The postmodern mind recognizes the validity of feelings, relationships, intuition, and experiences as a means to arriving at truth. The spiritual, which was often treated pejoratively by moderns, is esteemed once again in postmodernism. Furthermore, the abstract thought-based lecture as the primary mode to learning is replaced by more artistic means of communication such as story, metaphor, and film. Learning is more participative and experiential.

Second, truth moved from the abstract locale of one's mind, or propositional truths, to what is experienced in real life. For example, postmoderns are not impressed by the propositional truth that the church is "the Body of Christ." It is a meaningless thought if it isn't an embodied reality. In other words, if the church isn't functioning as the presence of Jesus in the world, doing what Jesus did, then it isn't true, or at least credible.

Third, the postmodern worldview replaces knowledge with interpretation. The same event can be seen differently depending on your vantage point. Therefore, truth can be plural. There may be several truths — truths that work for you and truths that work for me. Furthermore, it is arrogant and disrespectful to judge another's perception of truth. Seeking to canonize one's version of truth over another's is seen as a play for control, power, and domination. Some of the modern era's greatest injustices and tragedies were vindicated by such a mentality.

Finally, because postmodern truth is based in practical reality, it is also related to their preference for authenticity. Instead of focusing on what one should be, and therefore creating distance between one another, people should deal with their honest realities and open the door to experience greater connection and intimacy. Postmoderns are not looking for something to believe in as much as a community in which to belong.

Three Tributaries of Change

As I work with youth ministry leaders and pastors throughout the country, they have been experiencing the impact of living in a postmodern world and, at the same time, they hunger to make a difference but sometimes feel stuck in the victim or survivor mode.

Part of the reason is that we haven't fully recognized three tributaries of change that have formed and converged into a Niagara Falls force over the past several decades.

1. From Modernism to Postmodernism

On March 27, 1964, the largest recorded earthquake in North American history ravaged Alaska. Lasting a full five minutes and measuring a 9.2 on a seismograph, the earthquake not only caused extensive damage, but also twisted the terrain. Neighborhoods located off the coastline before the quake boasted of ocean views afterwards. Similarly, over the past several decades, an epistemological earthquake has shaken our understanding of truth, our views, and our life perspectives. Our culture is transitioning from a modern to a postmodern world, and as a result we are seeing and understanding the world very differently than before.

Perhaps one of the most significant challenges to reaching the younger generation resides in the fact that we are living within an epistemological parenthesis. Our culture, including our Catholic culture, runs on two operating systems, an older modern platform and a newer postmodern version. Generally speaking, young people tend to be the early adopters, while older folks may stay with a system that's familiar and comfortable. More specifically, although highly concentrated in present-day teens, postmodernism's cultural influence spans multiple generations. Nevertheless, with two languages to describe and understand the world, the present generational disconnect lacks any mystery.

2. From Generation X to the Millennial Generation

In addition to an epistemological revolution, we are transitioning into a new generation of teens. In actual fact, the Millennial Generation teens (born from 1982 on) arrived in our parishes in 1995, and Gen Z (born after 2002) are on the horizon. Their incursion brought an entirely new meaning to the term "generation gap." Prior to this time, a "generation gap" described the differing values, views, and misunderstandings between teens and their parents. Today, it represents the gap between what adults think is true about teens and what is actually true.

I often include a twenty-question opening quiz on the traits and trends of the Millennial Generation when giving presentations. The vast majority of parents, catechists, and youth ministers fail with dismal scores well below fifty percent. The fact is Millennial Generation teens are very distinct from their Boomer and Generation X predecessors. Many of our common assumptions don't work with this cohort. Furthermore, many of our established and current youth ministry practices (built on those assumptions) were developed during the late Baby Boomers (born 1943–1960) and Generation X (born 1961–1981) teen years. The result is the polite disinterest and disconnect from our present ministerial efforts.

3. From the Print Era to Electronic/Digital Communications

The Western world has traversed through three major eras in communication: Oral, Print, and Electronic/Digital. Each era provides a certain lens in which one experiences and understands the world. The oral culture was based upon the spoken word. People, gathered in community, learned through storytelling, retelling, shared experiences, conversations, and ritual. Taught through mentoring, oral learners learned via discipleship or apprenticeship.

The Print era took full form in 1438 with the invention of the Gutenberg press. By the sixteenth century, Europe had over nine million books in circulation, laying an academic minefield to be fully detonated during the intellectual explosion of the Renaissance and Scientific Revolution. "Print technology," states David Lochhead, was "the catalyst that allowed the emerging mechanistic, linear, individualistic tendencies of the modern period to become the integrated, dominant pattern of its time."[10] Learning shifted from mentoring through relationships and community to reading, individual study, and lecture — hence the modern classroom.

The Electronic era began with telephone and radio, and quickly evolved into film and television. Today, digital technologies such as video games, computers, and high-speed

Internet converge words, sounds, images, and interactivity. Instead of primarily learning in linear fashion through reading, individual study, and lecture, the digital era explodes in every direction via hyperlinks, empowering the navigator to search and experience a ubiquitous stream of sights, sounds, and text. Gerard Kelly writes, "The shifting status of text is a key factor in the wave of social change currently transforming western culture. Whatever else the emerging generations will be, they will be post-literate. The Church, with its emphasis on text-as-truth, propositional teaching and word-only sermons, has hardly begun to explore this new ground. But explore it we must — it is the landscape into which we are moving."[11]

Today's teens are indigenous to the digital age. They think in hyperlink fashion, learn through participation, make decisions collaboratively, and access their information electronically. We cannot use yesterday's pastoral and catechetical approaches within today's environment without risking a major disconnect. We may have cut our catechetical teeth during the print dynasty (linear, systematic, propositional, and text-based), but we must resist the temptation to canonize past learning methodologies, mistakenly fusing them to the actual content of the faith. The challenge of transitioning to the electronic/digital age is learning to become more experiential, participatory, image-based, and connected.[12]

If you agree that the world has changed, culture has changed, and young people have changed, the obvious question is, "Why is this so important?" According to RDR Group's research (a consulting firm that provides training to high-level corporate and nonprofit groups), "In a changing world, it is not the strongest organization, nor the one with the most knowledge that survives; it is the one most resilient to change." The RDR Group defines resilience as the ability to foresee, adapt, learn, and benefit from change with speed and agility. In addition, it identified three common responses to change: 1) Becoming a victim, "There's nothing I can do"; 2) Being a survivor, "That's just the way it goes"; or 3) Being a navigator, "I can make a difference; here's what I can do."

Management researcher and author Jim Collins (author of *Build to Last* and *Good to Great*) says that leaders should resist the tendency to slip into denial as a coping mechanism when dealing with change. According to Collins, facing the truth head on is a very first important step in dealing with change and can be a matter of survival.

It is my hope that by working together, we can become more resilient in dealing with the changes we face in Catholic youth ministry. Let's start with the first step of facing the reality of today's teens, parents, and current trends in parish life.

Scheme of a Teen?

Projected on the screen behind me were the words, "Our civilization is doomed if the unheard-of actions of our younger generations are allowed to continue." I asked the group of parents, catechists, and youth ministers, "Who do you think wrote or coined this phrase?"

"My pastor after our last youth lock-in," quickly confessed one sheepish youth minister.

"My dad said stuff like that all time," moaned a younger parent.

Russ, a very wise volunteer youth minister in a small parish, shook his head and said, "That's got to be the first hieroglyphics known to mankind!" He wasn't far from the truth. They weren't hieroglyphics, but cuneiform characters expressing the sentiments of an elder in the Sumerian city of Ur, around 2000 B.C.

> We commonly assume the present generation is an extension of the previous generation, only worse. Etched into ancient tablets and probably in our very DNA are sentiments about youth like these: "The children now love luxury; they have bad manners, contempt for authority; they show disrespect for elders ... are now tyrants. They contradict their parents,... and tyrannize their teachers" (attributed to Socrates, fifth century B.C., and echoed in some form by every adult generation since). It's safe to say that we've successfully transitioned into adulthood when we begin to critique present youth as worse than our own generation was when we were teens.

Yes, youth and trouble have been synonymous terms for centuries, even millennia. That's why few were shocked when eighteen-year-old Scotty Davis, Jr., was arrested for building numerous pipe bombs in a Columbine-style plot targeting his old high school. After all, he was a troubled teen. He was being treated for depression, and involuntarily committed to a mental health facility the previous year. Furthermore, he was expelled from Pace-Brantley Hall School months earlier. Thank God, fifty-year-old Ken Reeves blew the whistle, revealing to Orange County deputies that Scotty disclosed to him his plan to blow up his former school and actually showed him where the explosive devices were hidden. On May 11, 2007, deputies apprehended the would-be villain and the school was saved from unspeakable disaster.

Scotty Davis, Jr., would be just another "youth gone wild" story except for the fact that he was framed. It turned out that Scotty's mother spurned Ken Reeves' romantic advances, and craving revenge, he entrapped her troubled son. Reeves assembled the bombs and hid them on the Davis's property, and then, like a hero, alerted the police.[13] Who would ever guess that this was not the scheme of a young teen, but the plan of a grown man? It's easy, almost natural, to blame teens. But are teens really the issue? Does the Church have a teen problem? One might think so when *glancing* over recent research.

The National Study of Youth and Religion

The 2003 *National Study of Youth and Religion* (NSYR) was the largest and most comprehensive research conducted on adolescents and faith in the United States. The ecumenical study issued a verdict on Catholic teens that was anything but flattering. In the words of lead researcher and author Christian Smith, "American Catholic teenagers appear to be faring particularly poorly, particularly badly. Catholic teenagers stood out to us as exceptionally weak in their faith, disengaged from the Church, and largely indifferent to faith and practice matters. By the hopes, standards, expectations, and so on of the Church itself for its young people, U.S. Catholic youth are doing, I think, remarkably badly."[14]

Smith was referencing the fact that Catholic teens consistently scored five to twenty-five percentage points below their Protestant peers in measures of religious belief, experiences and activities.[15] Furthermore, Smith found that many Catholic teens were living far outside the norms of Catholic teaching. For instance, only 10 percent of Catholic teens reported that religion was "extremely important" in shaping their daily lives. Compare that with 20 percent of mainline Protestant teens, 29 percent of conservative Protestant teens, and 31 percent of black Protestant teens who felt that way. Furthermore, the NSYR reports that Catholic teens lack a general knowledge and understanding of Catholic beliefs and doctrines. On a whole, Catholic teens were quite inarticulate in explaining the Church's teachings.

Once the interviews for NSYR study concluded, the seventeen team members gathered for a week of debriefing. Christian Smith described the moment, "We all basically looked at each other and said, 'What is up with the Catholic teenagers?'"[16]

That "what's up with the Catholic teenagers" landed us our own chapter in Soul Searching,[17] a book written by Christian Smith and Melinda Lundquist Denton, revealing the findings of the National Study of Youth and Religion. Maybe it's nothing to brag about, but the chapter did help clarify why Catholics scored lower than their protestant peers.

NSYR research discovered that such differences "can be significantly explained by the lower levels of religiosity of their parents" when those parents are compared with Protestant parents. Notably, the parents of the Catholic teens are far less likely than their Protestant counterparts to participate in organized parish activities outside worship.[18]

In other words, our issue is less about Catholic teens than it is about the adult Church in general since youth, more often than not, reflect the religious commitment of their parents. Consequently, we do not have a teenage problem as much as we have an ecclesial or entire church problem. More importantly, NSYR research clearly demonstrates that parents are the most significant religious influence in their children's lives. For example, of parents who indicate that their faith is extremely important in their daily lives, 67 percent of their teenage children report that their faith is extremely or very important in their daily lives. Of those same parents, only 8 percent of their teens report that their faith was not very or not at all important in their daily lives. For the middle of the road parents who reported that their faith is somewhat important to their daily lives, sixty-one percent of their teenage children indicated the same — that their faith is somewhat important or not very important to their daily lives. Only eight percent of their children claimed that their faith was extremely important in their daily lives. On the lower end of the spectrum, of parents who reported that their faith was not at all important in their daily lives, forty-seven percent of their children state that their faith was not very or not at all important in their daily lives. Only two percent of their teens state faith is extremely important to their daily lives.[19]

Smith and Denton conclude:

> Contrary to popular misguided cultural stereotypes and frequent parental misconceptions, we believe that the evidence clearly shows that the single most important social influence on the religious and spiritual lives of adolescents is their parents. Grandparents and other relatives, mentors, and youth workers can be very influential as well, but normally, parents are most important in forming their children's religious and spiritual lives. Teenagers do not seem very reflective about or appreciative of this fact. But that does not change the reality that the best social predictor, although not a guarantee, of what the religious and spiritual lives of youth will look like is what the religious and spiritual lives of their parents *do* look like. Parents and other adults most likely 'will get what they are.' This recognition may be empowering to parents, or alarming, or both. But it is a fact worth taking seriously in any case. [20]

Shocked by the Obvious

From the onset, the Scriptures emphasize the essential role of parents in passing on the faith to children. "These commandments that I give you today are to be upon your hearts. Impress them on your children. Talk about them when you sit at home and when you walk along the road, when you lie down and when you get up" (Deuteronomy 6:6–7). Furthermore, throughout history the Church has consistently affirmed the family as the primary context for faith development.[21]

Yet, somehow contemporary adults find this a bit startling. Baby Boomer and Gen X parents remember their own teen years, and hope to God there's no truth to karma! Teen Boomers rebelled against their parents and the establishment while Gen X teens felt ignored by both and retreated to their own peer worlds. The Baby Boomers famous credo, "Never trust anyone over thirty," helped bring intergenerational programming to extinction or at least on the endangered list. Any parish making an honest attempt at reaching Boomers and Gen X teens developed youth programming that segregated adolescents from the adult population. The only exceptions were a few cool adults who helped lead the group. (A "cool adult" was defined as an adult who was not one of your parents.)

Often, Boomer and Gen X parents assume from their own experience that they have little influence on their adolescent children and the best way to reach teens is to segregate them from the adult church. Most parishes still hum along this well-worn road with little thought or concern. But this default route is paved with outdated assumptions. Millennial Generation teens are not rebelling against authority or their parents. They actually like their parents and are quite comfortable with adults. Ask a group of teens to name their heroes and you'll be told the same names over and over — "my mom" or "my dad." Add to the equation that parents are the most significant influence in their teenage children's lives, and the need to expand the borders of youth ministry becomes quite obvious. Parents need a lot more of our pastoral attention years before their children reach adolescence. These connections and bonds need to be established when their children are young or even prior to the birth of children. Otherwise, we risk losing the hearts of parents and consequently their children's.

Don't Blame Parents

When we trace the path of today's Catholic teens' commitment, it ends with parents. Consequently, religious educators may be tempted to affix their scope and center their crosshairs on religiously listless parents. "If they only valued Mass or the Church as much as the athletic involvements of their children," we commonly lament. Or, we blame the "fluff" of post-Vatican II religious education that many of today's parents received as the culprit. But in either case, we would only further alienate parents and anesthetize ourselves from the real story.

On the whole, we can't accuse parents of today's teens of not wanting what's best for their kids. Notorious for their parental overinvolvement and ever hovering, they merit the title "helicopter parents." They shell out small fortunes and invest countless hours to ensure that their children are highly skilled and involved athletically, artistically, or academically. So, why are they not doing the same for their kids spiritually?

Conditioned by their own parish experience, parents may see little practical benefit in church commitment, apart from being a sacramental provider for their children. Many may feel spiritually undernourished and under-challenged themselves. Others may question the practical relevancy of the Church after consuming a steady diet of homilies that emphasize what we believe (doctrine) rather than how we should live (practical application). Not experiencing a strong relational attachment to their parish, perhaps they have found community and a deeper emotional connection within other contexts such as their children's school or sports circles. Not experiencing a strong sense of vision or mission in their parish, parents may have found one in their children's activities or competitive endeavors. In other words, parents are what they are because the Church is what she is.

The fact is we have failed to engage parents. For many, the fullness of the Catholic faith has been distilled down to a fraction of its richness: getting their children through the motions of the initiation sacraments. In the end, when parents feel they receive little from their parish, they tend to give little back in return — and that exchange often becomes their children's spiritual inheritance.

Some may argue that this sounds a lot more like self-fulfillment than self-sacrifice. Aren't we only transferring our consumerist values as a society to church involvement? Shouldn't we attend church to worship God? Isn't church about what we give rather than what we receive?

Being an active member of a church and getting nothing in return sounds wonderfully pious, but lacks any basis in human reality. People are much more willing to give their time, talents, and treasure to organizations from which they feel they are receiving something valuable in return. That return rarely originates from a "What's in it for me?" motivation. Rather, their return is a natural response from what they believe they have received. Maybe that's what Jesus was getting at when he said, "From everyone who has been given much, much will be demanded; and from the one who has been entrusted with much, much more will be asked" (Luke 12:48). Perhaps some parishes experience the converse of this passage, where little is given and little is returned.

An army sent into battle without food, proper equipment, and the supplies needed to prevail will suffer from low morale, high attrition, and frequent defections. Over time soldiers feel used, uncared for, and disillusioned with their government — hardly the ingredients for a successful campaign and later re-enlistment. On the other hand, the motivation for self-sacrifice flows from a well-cared-for platoon. The Apostle John said, "We love because he first loved us" (1 John 4:19). When loved by Christ — through his living body, the Church — we tend to love in response. In the end, the real story is not about teens, the failure of modern adolescent catechesis, or youth ministry. In many ways it's not even about parents. It's about something much larger.

The Elephant in the Pew

There's an elephant crowding the pews of many Catholic sanctuaries. Most see it, but don't address it. Maybe we've simply become accustomed to it. Maybe it's been a part of our spiritual landscape for so long that it has blended into the design of the stained glass. Maybe we're afraid we will appear weird, disrespectful, or unfaithful if we honestly describe what we see.

When it comes to elephants, it's better to be a child. Children clearly notice and rudely point out unusual things like out-of-place beasts. Our children have identified the elephant in the sanctuary when they groan on Sunday morning, saying, "I don't want to go to church, it's soooo boring." Or "Religious education is a waste of my time. We only repeat the same stuff over and over." But children don't know what's good for them, we reassure ourselves, and church is good for them.

Yet, if we pause long enough and take a painfully honest look at our overall parish experience, perhaps we may agree with our children? Sure it's impolite and even ecclesiologically incorrect to say, "I am bored by Mass" or "I don't get anything out of church." Not only is it impolite, we may also feel guilty saying it. Echoing through our consciences are rebuttals like, "You only get out of Mass what you put into it." Or "You're are not there to take, but to give." Those pious platitudes have given the elephant free reign in the sanctuary. They have anchored us into the religious status quo. And, the results are telling: many Catholics have quietly left our ranks. Some simply don't attend church. Others have found friendlier spiritual homes outside the Catholic tradition. Many of those who remain are indifferent and spiritually stagnant. I am not sure if "no pain, no gain" works in this context.

This certainly does not represent every American Catholic's experience. There are many vibrant, alive, and spiritually engaging parishes. Furthermore, this is not an indictment against Catholic pastoral leaders — many who have invested their entire lives to the Church at great personal sacrifice. As one of those leaders, I understand the frustration and discouragement that accompanies exhaustive efforts with little return. Sometimes, my first inclination is to blame the very people I am called to serve. Better sense comes my way when I imagine Coke's board of directors trying to shame members of the public for switching to Pepsi because they were dissatisfied with Coke. Likewise, as pastoral leaders, we must avoid the occupational hazard of blaming the very people we are called to serve. Sure, chronic complainers exist, but they can't be our excuse for not listening to those we serve. And yes, there are religious consumers, but they consume because they are hungry and searching for more. Our culture has changed, and we are called to feed and serve people by meeting them where they are.

The Terrain Has Changed

Postmodern times altered the spiritual palates of many Catholics. People do not come to Mass to learn the attributes of God as much as to experience the living presence of God. They don't want to leave with a cerebral moment as much as being moved by the moment. In the modern era one was suspect of emotions. In a postmodern era emotions are a significant indicator of authentic engagement. This is not to say that great liturgy stimulates the tear ducts, while flatlining the brain waves. Great liturgy stimulates the whole person — mind, body, and emotions.

Furthermore, many Catholics hunger for a deeper experience of real community. Attending Mass surrounded by a sea of anonymous, disconnected faces does nothing to stimulate an emotional bond with fellow parishioners. It's unrealistic to expect to know every face and name in larger parishes, yet people need meaningful relationships with at least some members of the congregation to feel like a part of the community. The more members feel like they belong, the deeper they will believe and commit.

Reaching teens isn't just about connecting with teens. It's about the very life and vitality of our parishes. Ignoring this pastoral reality while attempting to spiritually reach teens is like sweeping the floor of a house that is completely submerged in flames.

FOR CONSIDERATION

- When it comes to change in your parish, which model do you see most often in parishioners?

    A) Victim: "There's nothing I can do."

    B) Survivor: "That's just the way it goes."

    C) Navigator: "I can make a difference; here's what I can do."

- What category do your parish leaders, including your pastor, fall into?

- What are some practical first steps you might take in order to become a navigator? How can you help convince victims and survivors that it is possible to become navigators?

- The National Study on Youth and Religion research concluded that parents are the single most important social influence on the religious and spiritual lives of their children. On a 1 to 10 scale (1 being low and 10 being high), how well does your parish reflect the priority of parent ministry? On a 1 to 10 scale how effective are you in reaching, supporting, and equipping parents in their role as primary religious educator of their children? List specific ways your parish responds.

- In what ways can your parish begin to make connections and support parents? What are some of the natural connection points that you can build upon? Are you utilizing these connections?

- What do you feel hinders parents from becoming fully invested in parish life in your faith community? In what ways do you address these obstacles?

Notes

10. David Lochhead, *Technology and Interpretation: A Footnote to McLuhan.* Journal of Theology. Dayton: United Theological Seminary, 1994.

11. Gerard Kelly, Trends. Posted at http://langleyvineyard.com/?p=448.

12. Leonard Sweet's acronym EPIC is detailed in his book *Post-Modern Pilgrims.* B & H Publishing Group, Nashville, 2000.

13. http://www.clickorlando.com/news/13432628/detail.html Police: Former Deputy 'Framed' Teen After His Mom Rejected Romantic Advances Teen Originally Accused Of Planning Va. Tech-Style Attack POSTED: Saturday, June 2, 2007 UPDATED: 9:44 am EDT June 4, 2007.

14. Fordham Center on Religion and Culture, November 2, 2006, 5:30 p.m.-7:30 p.m. Fordham University, New York, New York.

15. *Soul Searching: The Religious and Spiritual Lives of American Teenagers,* Christian Smith with Melinda Lundquist Denton, Oxford University Press, 2005. Page 194.

16. Fordham Center on Religion and Culture, November 2, 2006, 5:30 p.m.-7:30 p.m. Fordham University, New York, New York.

17. *Soul Searching: The Religious and Spiritual Lives of American Teenagers,* Christian Smith with Melinda Lundquist Denton, Oxford University Press, 2005.

18. Ibid.

19. Ibid., pages 56-57.

20. Ibid., page 261.

21. *Code of Canon Law,* Can. 774 §2; *Catechism of the Catholic Church* 2225, 2226; *A Family Perspective in Church and Society* (1988); *Follow the Way of Love* (1994).

CHAPTER TWO

MILLENNIALS AND GEN Z

"Coop! Coop! Coop!" screamed the Elgin Maroons' student body. From the sidelines, the opposing Lake Park Lancers' football players and coach gave "Coop" a stirring ovation as he pointed his finger up, saluting them. Winfred Cooper was celebrating the best day of his eighteen years.

Earlier that September day in the Chicago suburbs, during the junior varsity game, opposing Lancer head coach, Nana Agyeman, noticed number 80 occasionally in the game and lining up far off the line of scrimmage. Learning from Elgin Maroon coach Dave Bierman that the player was Cooper, a rarely used senior with severe autism, he offered, "Well, if you want to throw him the ball, just let us know."

Concocted by coaches from both teams during half time, the Driver-Driver play was called from the huddle. The quarterback rolled out under pressure and lobbed a wobbly pass in Cooper's direction. Cringing, the coaches followed the pass to the open arms of Cooper. He pulled in the ball and began to sprint madly towards the goal line. "Out running" the entire defense and dodging one well-choreographed tackle attempt from an opposing defender, Winfred scored a sixty-seven yard touchdown. Pandemonium broke out in the end zone, in the stands, and on both sidelines. Coaches from both teams choked back tears as they watched Cooper perform his signature dance known as the "Winfred Shuffle."

Some of his teammates even danced with him in this "Rudy"-like moment. Cooper wasn't letting go of that ball, either![22]

The Lancers eventually won the game by a touchdown, but the most important victory was the moment in Winfred Cooper's life. Everyone on both sides of the field shared in his triumph.

Meet the Millennials

Welcome to the Millennial Generation. This scenario would have little chance of materializing with previous teenage generations. Teenage Boomers and Gen Xers worked more from the Vince Lombardi maxim: "Winning isn't everything. It's the only thing."[23] Growing up during an era when trophies were earned by simply being a part of the team, regardless of one's skill, Millennials better understand the importance of working together and supporting one another. Understanding their social location, perspectives, and distinguishing characteristics are important prerequisites for reaching them. Of course, like members of any generation, not all Millennial Generation teens fit neatly within the following descriptions; however, each generation shares a social biography and cultural experiences that influence common views and shaped beliefs.

Let's look at some of the features that help define the Millennial Generation personality.

The first Millennial Generation teens entered our parish high school youth ministries and religious education programs around 1996. Take the following quiz to assess your knowledge of Millennial Generation teens and basic youth trends.

TABLE 1: *Millennial Generation Quiz*[24]

Place an X in the box that you think best reflects the direction of the following youth trends since 1995. Afterwards, check your answers on page 44 (Table 2).

Teen Behavior or Characteristic since 1995	Up	No Change	Down
1. Percentage who had sexual inter-course			
2. Had sexual intercourse with a total of four or more partners			
3. Engaged in a physical fight in the last 12 months			
4. Carried a weapon to school in the last month (gun, knife, club)			
5. Driving after drinking alcohol			
6. Percentage who drink any alcohol			
7. Binge drinking			
8. Percentage who used marijuana at least once			
9. Percentage to ever smoke cigarettes			
10. Teen birthrate (14–18 years old)			
11. Abortion rate			
12. Suicide rate			
13. Violent crime in schools			
14. School shooting fatalities (grade/secondary schools)			
15. School dropout rate			

What makes the Millennial Generation different? Let's begin by seeing how you did on the quiz (Table 1).

TABLE 2: *Millennial Generation Quiz*[25]

Teen Behavior or Characteristic since 1995	Up	No Change	Down
1. Percentage who had sexual intercourse			X
2. Had sexual intercourse with a total of four or more partners			X
3. Engaged in a physical fight in the last 12 months			X
4. Carried a weapon to school in the last month (gun, knife, club)			X
5. Driving after drinking alcohol			X
6. Percentage who drink any alcohol			X
7. Binge drinking			X
8. Percentage who used marijuana at least once			X
9. Percentage to ever smoke cigarettes			X
10. Teen birthrate (14–18 years old)			X
11. Abortion rate			X
12. Suicide rate			X
13. Violent crime in schools			X
14. School shooting fatalities (grade/secondary schools)			X
15. School dropout rate			X

In chapter one, I mentioned that the majority of training participants who take the quiz on Millennials score below 50 percent. Whether you smoked it or bombed it, there's much to learn about the Millennials.

The Millennial Generation is presently the largest generation in U.S history, with over 80 million strong, eclipsing the size of the Baby Boomers. When factoring in immigration, some experts estimate their size will reach 100 million.[26] The most ethnically diverse generation in American history, over 40 percent of Millennials are non-white or Latino.

They are also known as Gen Y (Y comes after X), the Net Generation, the Digital Generation (growing up as Internet and digital natives), or the Echo Boomers (because of the growing birth rate to Boomer mothers),[27] and more recently Gen We (because of their tendency towards teamwork). But, according to several surveys, they overwhelmingly prefer the title "Millennials." The title was coined in 1988 as they entered kindergarten, anticipating their high school graduation date of 2000.

TABLE 3: *American Generations*

Generation Name	Birth Years
G.I. Generation	1901 – 1924
Silent	1925 – 1942
Baby Boomers	1943 – 1960
Generation X	1961 – 1981
Millennials/Gen Y	1982 – 2002
iGeneration/Gen Z	2003 –

Who Are the Millennials?

The Millennial Generation heralds an impressive array of descriptive titles such as the "Good News Generation," the "Sunshine Generation," and the "Next Great Generation."

The "Good News" title is not without warrant. As the previous quiz answers indicate, negative trends of previous teenage generations have declined. Comparing figures from the 1995 and 2009 *US Youth Risk Behavior Surveillance Report*, today's high school students are less likely to have had sexual intercourse (down 7.1%); to have had sexual intercourse with four or more partners (down 5%); to have been in a physical fight (down 7.2%); to have carried a weapon to school (down 4.2%); to have driven after drinking alcohol (down 5.7%); to have ridden with a driver who had been drinking alcohol (down 10.5%); to have ever drank alcohol (down 7.9%); to have ever drank alcohol before thirteen years old (down 11.3%); to have drunk alcohol in the past 30 days (down 9.8%); to have been binge drinking in the past 30 days (down 8.4%); to have ever used marijuana (down 5.6%); to have used marijuana in the past 30 days (down 4.5%); to have ever smoked cigarettes (down 25%); to have smoked a cigarette before thirteen years old (down 14.2%); to have been a frequent smoker (down 8.8%); to have seriously considered suicide during the past twelve months (down 10.3%); to have experienced violent crime in schools (down over 50%);[28] to have experienced school shooting fatalities (95–96 school year: 29; 2009–10 school year: 5)[29].[30]

In 2009, the US birthrate among 15- to 19-year-old girls was recorded at 39.1 births per 1,000 teenagers. This number is the lowest number recorded in the almost seventy years of the U.S. government tracking teenage childbearing. In 1991, during the Gen X teen years, the overall 15- to 19-year-old birthrate stood at over 60 births per 1,000 teenagers.[31] Furthermore, violent crime, suicides,[32] and abortions have all declined with this generation.[33]

There may be a combination of influences, factors, or causal directions leading to the decrease of many negative teenage behaviors. We cannot, however, explain away the fact that almost across the board teens are engaging less in risky behaviors. Actually, it should come as no surprise.

The Millennials arrived during a time when America was quite positive about children. The "No Children Allowed" warnings surrendered to the minivan alerts of "Baby on Board." Many educational and social initiatives were launched in order to reverse some of the negative trends that besieged the youth of previous generations. Churches got on board by hiring youth ministers and developing youth ministries. Schools developed policies that ensured that every student had equal access to an education. The Millennials enjoyed unprecedented focus, protection, and positive opportunities.

Within a single generation, kids morphed from having the reputation of raising themselves to being mega-managed by ever-hovering parents. Behind many Millennial students and athletes stand highly invested parents. For many teachers, coaches, and youth ministers, their most difficult challenges are no longer the children, but their entangled parents. As Millennials entered college, universities responded to this new breed of parent by creating new departments that address parental relations and concerns (so that's why tuition keeps rising!).

Core Characteristics of Millennial Teens

The following section looks at five core Millennial characteristics and the practical implications for those ministering to youth. Once again, it must be noted that these traits may not be true for every Millennial teen.

1. They Are Special and Hovered Over

While conducting a parish focus group with senior high Millennials, I heard a young man grumble that his pastor doled out to him the same penance given to his peers. A symphony of protests made it clear that this was an unacceptable pastoral practice! It was as if the seniors were saying, "I'm a unique sinner who deserves a unique penance!" Furthermore, they felt it was a reasonable expectation for their pastor to greet them by name on Sunday mornings.

This shouldn't be a surprise. Millennials have been conditioned to feel special. (They routinely received trophies for participation; skill was not even an issue.) They are accustomed to being hovered over by their parents, and American society as a whole. They grew up during a period when children were the dominant political agenda and over time they absorbed that message. The old adage, "Children should be seen, but not heard" was sent hastily into retirement during the eighties. Children were not only seen and heard, but they were recorded and chronicled. Their video-toting parents were present at all of their childhood events (often beginning at birth). The parental (and video) lens was always firmly focused on their "stars," and the Millennial child adopted this metaphor for life. Not surprisingly, many Millennials have come to understand and expect that the parents' purpose in life is to be centered around the child's well-being, education, and future success.[34]

One might think all this pooled attention would produce a generation of highly selfish and self-absorbed kids. Not necessarily so. Millennials broke away from the individualistic focus of the Boomers and Gen Xers, turning instead on the collective good.

Isn't this tendency toward valuing the collective good and the underlying message that everyone is special an asset for youth ministry and the church as a whole? It is if we recognize the change in thinking and approach that it requires.

Traditionally, we've focused on the question, "What are we doing for our teens?" For Millennials, we need to shift the question towards, "How can Millennials be meaningfully involved in the Church?" We need to make important paradigmatic shifts, transitioning teens from merely objects of ministry to subjects of ministry as well. Opening the doors for meaningful involvement on every level of parish life is critical to keeping Millennials engaged in the church. Young people need to be invited and trained as greeters, Eucharistic ministers, lectors, ushers, and cantors. Furthermore, they need to work with adults, side by side in every ministry — where they contribute, learn from their elders, and build life-long intergenerational relationships. An essential question that every parish ministry group needs to ask is, "How can we integrate our young people into all we do?" Training every ministry leader and adult participant on how to relate to, support, mentor, and include young people is a critical step towards reaching this new generation. In many ways, we have to reorient ourselves into seeing youth as ministry apprentices and ourselves as mentors, gift discoverers, and skill developers. When we begin to operate on this level, young people will feel included and special in our community.

Conventional routes of invitation into the life and ministries of our faith community will not work with a "special" generation. Teens are neither impressed with nor persuaded by impersonal and routine invitation, which tends to be business as usual for many Catholic parishes (e.g., bulletin, mail, Mass announcements). While conducting focus groups with teens, they've conceded to me that they hear the Mass announcements inviting them to be involved. However, they rarely consider what they impersonally hear. Their parents and much of society have conditioned them to higher expectations. When a church doesn't behave similarly (or a step above), teens may perceive this lack of attention as uncaring. Our invitations must be personal and even better, given within an established relationship through someone who actually knows their names. Old-fashioned hospitality helps teens feel like they belong, are wanted, and have a place among us.

2. They Value Relationships

Millennial teens highly value relationships with their family and friends. Topping the list of most the important priorities in their lives, young adult Millennials named being a good parent, having a successful marriage, and helping others in need. All three relational priorities eclipsed preferences such as high paying careers, lots of free time, and becoming famous.[35]

In recent years, many parishes and dioceses have experienced dwindling attendance for large group events such as rallies and youth conferences. These declines may reflect Millennials' preference for engaging experiences within smaller more intimate settings. The large events in which today's teens remain attracted feature interactive speakers and activities, along with opportunities to connect with others on a deeper level.

Millennials highly value relationships and respond very favorably when caring adults invest in getting to know them. Furthermore, possessing relationships with significant adults in one's faith community increases a teen's chances towards developing a committed young adult faith.[36] The very best ministries with young people are constructed beneath a web of deep and meaningful relationships. Programs, classes, and events can never substitute for the life-on-life intersection of real relationships.

In an extensive Group/Youth for Christ survey, teenagers indicated that relationships with adult Christians and parents were most influential in their initial decision to follow Christ: "It's people who live out their relationship with God in a real way who make a difference in teenagers spiritual growth. Teens grew when they were immersed in the disruptive, emotional, surprising realm of real relationships."[37] Additionally, youth ministers were asked what led them to commit their lives to Christ when they were young, and later their decision to enter youth ministry. Rick Lawrence reports:

> Everyone we interviewed said all the defining moments in the path toward Christian maturity were relational. For one it was a late-night talk with an adult volunteer in a tent. For another it was a youth minister who believed in him enough to give him leadership responsibilities.
>
> Here's the surprising thing; these people were impacted most by the tiny, nondescript things adult and teenage Christians did for them. They were most powerfully influenced when other Christians revealed a kind of spontaneous Christ-likeness in the context of relationship. It wasn't the well-planned, well-presented teaching series on Colossians that changed their life. It was the tears welling up in their leader's eyes when he listened to their struggles. And 20 years later, they still remember those eyes and those tears.[38]

Much of today's parish youth ministry, while espousing in theory the value of significant relationships (with adults), seems, in practice, to operate in large-group programs. While there could be many reasons, one has been the reaction to the sexual abuse crises.

Many effects of the abuse crises are easily evident. The obvious damage includes unspeakable pain for the children abused, the disillusionment of many Catholics, billions in legal costs, and the subsequent budget cuts that again affected children by reducing or eliminating needed ministry services. In the end, however, what may be of more damage to youth ministry (and to the Church) may be something designed to be a very positive response to the sexual abuse crises — our protection policies. In an effort to protect young people, the responses we have formed through legal policies and guidelines may be hampering, limiting, challenging (and perhaps even driving to extinction) significant relational ministry. These policies often wind up protecting teens from much more than predators. In the end, we protect them from any meaningful contact with adults. The result is that Millennials highly value relationships and are quite comfortable with adults, yet adult church leaders are afraid to get too close to teens. Many good and healthy priests, youth ministers, and volunteer leaders have become reluctant to engage teens outside the formality of programs. But misinterpreting safe to mean stepping out of teens' lives and pruning our roles down to paper and program management is a costly mistake. Many leaders, primarily operating from a spirit of fear, have sanitized humanity from ministry by prohibiting any meaningful interpersonal contact. Again, don't misunderstand me — we must vigilantly protect teens through safe, appropriate, and prudent practices — but let's not sterilize our impact in the process. Teens need meaningful relationships with significant adults in order to grow spiritually.

Church leaders, as good stewards, do need to guard against further financial losses that would negatively impact many forms of ministry. However, overly stringent policies lead to a Church that is more concerned about financial and legal protection than on the active, personal, pastoral care of young people. This results in the loss of the Church's credibility and the far greater loss of our teens.

I don't want to address a highly complex and deeply challenging situation by offering simplistic platitudes. I am in no way suggesting we ignore policies, but we need to advocate for more reasonable expression that both protects and positively impacts teens. It is time for "protection and prevention" to meet "practical and pastoral." In the end, we must discover our true identity, a holy Church led by the Spirit, where the call to love precedes a preoccupation about liability.

3. They Are Close To Their Parents

Millennials tend to like their parents! More than one in three teens (35 percent) characterize their relationship with their mothers as "extremely close." Among African American mothers, that number swells to 45 percent. Over 41 percent of teens report feeling "extremely close" to their fathers.[39] Over 90 percent report that they "trust" and "feel close" to their parents.[40] Their parents are more likely to be reported as their heroes than any other person. Most identify with their parents' values. Contrast that with the teenage Boomers, when in 1974, a whopping 40 percent said, "That they would be better off living without their parents."[41]

The conversations parents are having with their teenage children are not the same conversations they had with their own parents when they were teens. Today, parents and their teens more freely discuss issues and topics that almost seemed taboo when they were growing up. A 2008 Teens Research Unlimited survey reported that 9 out of 10 teens say they're "close" to their parents; 75 percent say they "like to do things with their family" and 59 percent say family dinners are "in."[42]

4. They Want to Make a Difference

While leading a discussion with a dozen Millennial teens, I asked, "Do you feel your parish cares about you as teens?" One young man spoke for the crowd when he exclaimed, "They care if we come, but they don't care if we're involved." For many Millennials, going to church and sitting passively is not enough. A part of being "special" is having a special purpose or role in the community. Millennials believe that they have an important individual and collective purpose in the world. They want to make a difference. Parishes who fall short of offering teens ample opportunities for meaningful involvement will find an increasing number of disconnected youth. They are not content to wait until adulthood to be active in their faith communities and world.

Parishes often fail to capitalize on the Millennials' collective call to make a difference in the world. Let's face it — teens are not parading out of our pews, protesting, "You are asking too much from me!" We are guilty of asking so little that we bore them out of our assemblies. Successfully connecting with today's youth means planting seeds for big dreams. Rather than buckling for fear of the risks, we need to passionately challenge teens *because of the risk*. We need to dare young people with a Spirit-led vision that captures their imagination for making a collective difference in their world. We can unleash the incredible energy of this great generation by simply changing the lens in which we view them. When we begin seeing our young people as future Saints who are only in need of a parish leader who recognizes their potential and a community that collectively nurtures their calling, we are on our way to producing world-changers.

5. They Are Stressed Out

Millennials are high achievers. They spend more time studying[43] and take heavier course loads in school than previous generations. They are painfully aware that their present performance directly impacts their future opportunities. Past generations were anxious about nuclear war, violence, and AIDS. Today, the greatest source of anxiety for teens is their grades and getting into a good college.

With fierce competition for the best colleges, many teens overload on a four-course menu of academics, extracurricular activities, sports, and volunteerism. Many teens choose their multiple involvements based upon how it will look on their college resume. Remember the good old days when we complained, "If only we offered teens some positive options." Now with option overload we lament, "If they only had more free time to relax." To manage their busy schedules, many teens tote various organizers, once the exclusive appendage of the adult corporate world.

High school athletic success often hinges upon years of previous competitive experience in a sport, year-round weight training, summer camps, and off-season competition. An increasing number of high school athletes have personal trainers, private coaches, and even sport psychologists.

The amplification of involvement and achievement has come at a cost: tension and stress. Combining the pressure to get into the best colleges with today's technological opportunities, a concerning number of teens resort to academic cheating. A 2010 survey of 40,000 senior high students reported that 59 percent admitted cheating on a test at least once in the past year, while 34 percent did it over two times. One in three reported that they used the Internet to plagiarize an assignment.[44]

In 2010, UCLA's annual freshman survey found the self-rated emotional health among incoming college freshman to be at its lowest point since they began asking the question in 1985. Almost one in three seniors reported being frequently "overwhelmed by all I had to do." Young women reported experiencing stress in greater numbers than young men. Only 17.6 percent of the boys reported feeling "frequently" overwhelmed, while 38.8 percent of the girls felt this way.[45]

Ministry Implications

Many teens suffer with tension, pressure, and busyness as constant companions in their lives. As church, it's critical that we don't multiply their stress by heaping on more meaningless demands, burdens, and requirements. In a similar context, Jesus said to a spiritually overburdened audience, "Come to me, all you who are weary and burdened, and I will give you rest. Take my yoke upon you and learn from me, for I am gentle and humble in heart, and you will find rest for your souls. For my yoke is easy and my burden is light" (Matthew 11:28–30).

Maybe the best way to evangelize Millennials is by personally introducing them to a God who is bigger than their successes and failures within an authentic church community that offers refuge for their weary bodies, minds, and souls. Additionally, our Church's contemplative prayer tradition may be the best remedy for a busy, stressed-out teen. Not only

Intergenerational and Family Ministry

As a whole, our parishes would do well to focus less upon children and more upon families.

Millennials are not a rebellious generation who are seeking freedom from out-of-touch adults. From early childhood their lives were highly organized, supervised, and coached by their parents and other adults. They have grown accustomed to their parents' involvement and adult presence in their lives. The Millennial Generation is more open and receptive to intergenerational and family-oriented programs than previous youth generations. Most parishes would benefit by offering more of these kinds of activities.

Some common denominators among generations that translate into effective intergenerational activities include storytelling, bible stories, service ministry, music or singing, art projects, videos or movies, participative rituals, and prayer. Providing families with common experiences of faith and outreach creates a stronger bond among family members and creates a deeper sense of community with other members of the parish.

Be careful not to misinterpret Millennial Generation teens' comfort with their parents and adults by slashing all youth gatherings and only offering intergenerational and family activities. Young people also want and need to be gathered with one another. It's not about switching out the entire youth ministry menu as much as expanding it by adding some intergenerational and family variety.

do overstressed and under-rested Millennials need the spiritual rooting that a deep prayer life provides, but also cultivating these practices during the teen years is one of the most significant factors in developing a strong and committed young adult faith later. Christian Smith with Patricia Snell in *Souls in Transition* write, "Emerging adults who as teenagers engaged in frequent and regular personal prayer and reading of Scripture prove more likely than those who did not to continue on as more highly committed believers, more capable of resisting countervailing forces and mechanisms that would reduce their religious commitments and practices."[46] Taking the time as a community to learn, develop, and support one another in spiritual practices such as solitude, silence, centering prayer, adoration, Sabbath-keeping, *lectio divina*, etc., may be the most important investment we make for producing present and future dividends.

The Positive News

Ninety percent of Millennials describe themselves as "happy," "positive," and "confident."[47] They are more likely to volunteer than teenagers of previous generations. According to UCLA's American Freshman survey, 86.7 percent of incoming freshman in 2010 volunteered at least occasionally during their high school senior year (compare to 66 percent in 1989). Furthermore, 32.1 percent reported there is a "very good chance" they will participate in volunteer or community service work while in college. That percentage was the highest ever measured since the question was first asked in 1990, rising over 15 percent.[48]

Millennial teens' perspective on intelligence and academic attainment differs from other recent teen generations. Eighty percent of Millennials say, "It's cool to be smart."[49] Compare that with the most satisfied student during my senior year in high school. A wrestler, he proudly passed around his particularly noteworthy achievement of straight F's while all the smart kids were hiding their academic success in order to avoid the socially inept status that came with it.

Furthermore, Millennials are the most highly educated generation in U.S. history. From 2000 to 2008, postsecondary undergraduate enrollment surged by 24 percent.[50] Since 2000, high school graduation rates have risen[51] and dropout percentages have fallen. In 2008, the status dropout rate was 8 percent, down from 14 percent in 1980.[52] In general, dropout rates for Whites, Blacks, and Hispanics each declined between 1980 and 2008. The number of Millennials who have taken and passed Advanced Placement tests has doubled in the past decade.

Millennials, Race, and Ethnicity

As with every generation, Millennials demonstrate a wide spectrum of behaviors. In no way does a broad decrease in the use of drugs, alcohol, sex, and violence mean that we do not have a concerning number of teens engaging in negative behaviors. Behind every statistic stands very real people and just one teen involved in risky behavior is one too many.

White Teens

Although Millennial Generation teens share in some general characteristics and positive trends, there certainly remains uniqueness and variance among races and ethnicities. For instance, some may presume that minority teens would be at greater risk for substance abuse. Recent research points otherwise, as white teens are more likely than African American, Latino, and Asian teens to get drunk, regularly

Continued on next page

smoke cigarettes, or use marijuana.[53] Although white teens have a lower rate of sexual intercourse than African American teens, they have the highest rate of oral sex and are the most sexually active (sexual contact beyond kissing).[54] On average, white teens spend more time with their peers in unsupervised settings, thus increasing the likelihood of participating in some at-risk behaviors. White teens, particularly females, report feeling the most pressure to look perfect, and achieve more in school and in extracurricular activities.[55] Furthermore, white females are least likely to report being very happy with their body and physical appearance, suffering with the worst body image compared to females of other races.[56]

Latino Teens

First- and second-generation Latino teens do not enjoy the financial resources and educational opportunities of later generations, but draw benefits from being well integrated within family and community networks. Their intergenerational involvements serve as a support and protection from many of the behavioral risks of the dominant culture. These safeguards, however, tend to breakdown by the third generation. Third-generation Latino teens integrate more fully into the dominant culture. Unfortunately, they absorb the risks without reaping the benefits. Like the dominant white culture, they spend less time with their families and more unsupervised time with their peers. Consequently, they lose the support and protection from their families and communities, without yet securing the outside organizational supports of which white teens readily enjoy. The result is third-generation Latino teens experience the greatest risk for destructive behaviors. As a subgroup they are most likely to drink alcohol, smoke marijuana, and have sexual intercourse (seventeen-year-olds).[57]

African American Teens

Body image is less of an issue for African American teens. They are more likely to be happy with their physical appearance than white, Latino, and Asian youth.[58] More than other teens, they describe their relationships with their mother as extremely close. However, they are the least likely to describe the same closeness with their father and are the most likely to be raised in a single-mother household. They are also most likely to get into physical fight. Although the majority of African American teens are not having sex, they are more likely than other teens to have had sexual intercourse, sexual intercourse with multiple partners, contract an STD, and become pregnant.[59]

Asian Teens

Asian American teens are least likely to engage in at-risk behaviors such as regular cigarette smoking, or marijuana use. Ironically, Asian American teens are most likely to feel that sexual intercourse is morally okay, but least likely to be sexually involved.[60] They spend as much time with their friends as white teens, but are less influenced towards risky behaviors, even when integrated within non-Asian American peer groups who are involved in risky activities. They tend to abstain from risky behaviors as a result of strong parental influence and a pragmatic view of life (where engaging in risky activities would be harmful or jeopardize their future). They are least likely to have divorced parents.

Ministry to Parents

We keep circling back to a critical linchpin for effectively passing on the faith to the next generation: parents.

Parents are the single most important spiritual influence in their teenage children's lives. In *Souls in Transition*, Christian Smith speaks of the influence of strong parental religion during the teenage years as an important factor towards a stronger young adult faith. "Emerging adults who grew up with seriously religious parents are through socialization more likely (1) to have internalized their parents' religious worldview, (2) to possess the practical religious know-how needed to live more highly religious lives, and (3) to embody the identity orientations and behavioral tendencies toward continuing to practice what they have been taught religiously."[61]

A youth ministry with a well-developed plan in reaching, supporting, and equipping parents provides the soil for teen faith to grow. The faith values, instruction, modeling, and practices conveyed within the structure of everyday family life produce roots for a lasting faith. This means that the pastoral staff needs to collaborate to provide a vision of discipleship that effectively equips parents to authentically live their faith and naturally share their faith with their children.

We need to be on the side of parents. Seeing them as "a problem" is never a solution. Over the years, I've witnessed a number of well-intentioned religious educators who let their frustration with parents get the best of them. Instead of existing as an advocate for parents by embracing and accompanying them in their role, they become an adversary. I've grimaced more than once after hearing condescending remarks aimed at parents for not having their religious priorities in order.

More than anything else, parents want partners. Many feel alone as they struggle through the daily challenges of parenting. They need and respond well to supportive, caring coaches who walk alongside them during the journey. Parish leaders who offer this kind of encouragement along with the mutual support of fellow parents will never have to worry about reprimanding parents for missing Mass. Furthermore, intentionally establishing these connections as early as when parents bring their children to the parish for baptism, will help ensure that the faith community functions more as an authentic parish family.

Generation Z on the Horizon

The ministry game changed with Millennials and will change again when Gen Z teens (born from 2003) arrive in our high schools sometime around 2017. Tentatively named Gen Z or the iGeneration (because they are so media savvy), this emerging generation will have their own unique ways of seeing life, learning, etcetera. As youth ministers, we'll need to adapt to the changing tide, just as we need to now.

What should we expect? First, our population will continue to grow in racial and cultural diversity. Catholic parishes will especially include a strong Latino presence. Welcoming and engaging a diverse group of Catholics will be a key challenge for many parishes.

Secondly, the next generation is more at home with digital technology than any previous generation. Since birth, they have been surrounded in technology in such a way that it has become invisible. Some researchers have found that young people's brains have been rewired with a greater capacity for multitasking as a result of simultaneously juggling numerous digital gadgets. Gen Z will be more at home with the interactivity of the online and video gaming environment than with the passive and linear approach of broadcast television. Native content producers, they learn best in active, participative, and creative contexts. As older people love the feel of a book in their hand, Gen Z may prefer the feel of a digital reading device. Print technologies will increasingly give way to wirelessly accessed digital media that combines images, words, sound, video, and interactivity. Social media will be second nature, and to reach the most technologically savvy generation, we will need to shift our catechesis in a digital direction. Learning to utilize social networking, blogs, podcasts, and wikis (collaborative writing space where users read, edit, and add content) for learning, interacting, and communicating will be critical for connecting with Gen Z.

One of our greatest challenges will be keeping up with and adapting to the rapid changes in technology. As an institutional Church, we tend to move at a snail's pace. We routinely make pronouncements regarding issues and situations dating several centuries earlier. We can't keep that kind of pace and expect to be a relevant force in teens' lives today! Without a "rapid deployment force," we run the risk of a major disconnect with the upcoming iGeneration.

Ironically, these fast-paced technological developments will actually create a deeper hunger for high-touch, real relationships. As information becomes more easily accessible and ubiquitous, young people will contract inward towards circles of trusted relationships. Our parishes will need to be centers for authentic, face-to-face sharing, and supportive communities.

In the whirlwind of a rapidly transforming culture, we often stand oblivious to the uproar surrounding us. We blithely navigate from outdated maps when we need a GPS. Not only is our world transitioning from a modern to a postmodern perspective, we are undergoing generational change. Many of our present youth ministry assumptions, approaches, and methodologies originated during the Generation X teen years, and they simply do not meet the needs of Millennials or the approaching Gen Z teens. Parishes that take the time to understand their present-day teens and renavigate their ministries accordingly will awaken a sleeping giant of a generation — a generation that has the potential to be one of the greatest in Church history.

FOR CONSIDERATION

- What characteristics of the Millennial Generation do you think are the most important to recognize and address in your youth ministry?
- How do you perceive today's generation gap? What do you feel are the most significant issues between young people and their elders today?
- In what ways can you use the characteristics or differences among white, African American, Latino, and Asian teens to create more individualized outreach programs?
- How do the adults and pastoral staff in your parish generally see young people? How can adults and parish staff become more ministry mentors, gift discovers, and skill developers?
- On a 1 to 10 scale (1 being low and 10 being high), how would you rate your level of relational ministry with teens? What obstacles stand in the way to a greater practice of relational ministry? What practical steps can be taken to increase relational ministry with teens?
- Many youth ministries and religious education programs operate with a youth segregation assumption. If your par-

ish does, how can you begin to implement more intergenerational programs?

- In what ways could your parish capitalize on Millennial Generation teens' desire to make a difference in the world?
- In what practical ways is your faith community preparing for Gen Z?

Notes

22. http://football.dailyherald.com/story/?id=323321. Autistic player's dream comes true as he scores his first touchdown. By Jamie Sotonoff.

23. The quote is commonly attributed to the legendary Green Bay Packer coach, Vince Lombardi. However, he never actually said this. He said, "Winning isn't everything, but making the effort to win is."

24. The quiz was developed by comparing the 1995 and 2009 Centers for Disease Control and Prevention's Youth Risk Behavior Surveillance Summaries. Summaries can be accessed from: http://www.cdc.gov/mmwr/PDF/ss/ss4504.pdf. (1995) and http://www.cdc.gov/mmwr/preview/mmwrhtml/ss5905a1.htm (2009).

25. Ibid.

26. *Millennials and the Pop Culture*. Neil Howe and William Strauss, Life Course Associates, 2006. Page 57.

27. The reality is that the larger half of the generation have Gen X parents.

28. Ages 12 to 18 years old comparing 1995 to 2007. Source: http://youthviolence.edschool.virginia.edu/violence-in-schools/national-statistics.html.

29. Editorial note: The percentage drops are all net drops. They do not represent the percentage of decrease. For instance, if in 1995 10% of teens used cocaine and that number declined to 5% in 2010 the net drop is 5%, the percentage dropped 50%. These numbers can be expressed either way.

30. The National School Safety Center's Report on School Associated Violent Deaths. Can be viewed at: http://docs.google.com/viewer?a=v&pid=sites&srcid=c2Nob29sc2FmZXR5LnVzfG5zc2N8Z3g6–NWFlZDdjZjBjMGY1Yjc3Mw.

31. National Vital Statistics Report. Volume 59, Number 3. Births: Preliminary Data for 2009. December 21, 2010. http://www.cdc.gov/nchs/data/nvsr/nvsr59/nvsr59_03.pdf.

32. Since 1997, the suicide death rate of 15- to 24-year-olds declined from 11 to 10 per 100,000 population. Suicide is the third leading cause among this age group. Health United States 2010 Report. U.S. Department of Health And Human Services, http://www.cdc.gov/nchs/data/hus/hus10.pdf#listtables

33. *Millennials and the Pop Culture*. Neil Howe and William Strauss, Life Course Associates, 2006. Chapter 3.

34. This is more true of white Millennials than African American, Latino, Asian teens, who tend to carry on with greater reciprocity. See: *Growing Up in America. The Power of Race in the Lives of Teens*. Brad Christerson, Korie L. Edwards, and Richard Flory. Stanford University Press, 2010. Page 13.

35. Millennials. A Portrait of Generation Next. Pew Research Center. February 2010. Page 18.

36. *Souls in Transition. The Religious & Spiritual Lives of Emerging Adults*. Christian Smith with Patricia Snell. Oxford University Press, 2009. "A second factor associated with stronger emerging adult religion is the

teenager *having more adults in a religious congregation to whom he or she can turn for support, advice, and help.* One social causal mechanism that we think helps create this statistical association is a *heightened enjoyment of religious congregational participation.*" Direct quote, page 233.

37. Rick Lawrence. "What Really Impacts Kids' Spiritual Growth." *Group.* Feb. 95 page 19.

38. Rick Lawrence. "What Really Impacts Kids' Spiritual Growth" Group Feb. 95, pages 19-20.

39. *Growing Up in America. The Power of Race in the Lives of Teens.* Brad Christerson, Korie L. Edwards, and Richard Flory. Stanford University Press, 2010. Page 32.

40. *Millennials and the Pop Culture.* Neil Howe and William Strauss, Life Course Associates, 2006. Page 42.

41. Ibid., page 42.

42. *USA Today,* April 14, 2008.

43. Comparing 1980 to 2002 in amount of time doing homework. In 1980 29 percent of students did more than 5 hours of homework per week. In 2002 that percentage jumped to 63 percent. http://nces.ed.gov/programs/coe/2007/section3/table.asp?tableID=697.

44. Josephson Institute for Ethics. Accessed at: http://charactercounts.org/programs/reportcard/2010/installment02_report-card_honesty-integrity.html.

45. The American Freshmen: National Norms Fall 2010. Cooperative Institutional Research Program at the Higher Educational Research Institute at UCLA. "The percentage of students reporting that their emotional health was in the "highest 10%" or "above average" when compared to their peers dropped 3.4 percentage points from 2009, from 55.3% to 51.9%. Women were far less likely than men to report high levels of emotional health (45.9% versus 59.1%, a difference of 13.2 percentage points), although both dropped similar amounts from 2009." Quoted from page 6.

46. *Souls in Transition. The Religious & Spiritual Lives of Emerging Adults.* Christian Smith with Patricia Snell. Oxford University Press, 2009. Page 235.

47. *Millennials Rising.* Neil Howe and William Strauss. Vintage Books New York, 2000. Page 7.

48. The American Freshman: National Norms Fall 2010.

49. *Millennials and the Pop Culture.* Neil Howe and William Strauss. Life Course Associates, 2006. Quoted from page 44.

50. http://nces.ed.gov/pubs2010/2010028.pdf.

51. Ibid. The overall average freshman graduation rate increased from 71.7 percent in 2000–01 to 73.9 percent in 2006–07, but between 2004–05 and 2005–06 it decreased from 74.7 to 73.4 percent.

52. http://nces.ed.gov/fastfacts/display.asp?id=16.

53. *Growing Up in America. The Power of Race in the Lives of Teens.* Brad Christerson, Korie L. Edwards, and Richard Flory. Stanford University Press, 2010. Page 56.

54. Ibid., page 65.

55. Ibid., page 54.

56. Ibid., page 55.

57. Ibid., pages 56, 63.

58. Ibid., page 55.

59. Ibid., pages 63, 64.

60. Ibid., page 63.

61. *Souls in Transition. The Religious & Spiritual Lives of Emerging Adults.* Christian Smith with Patricia Snell. Oxford University Press, 2009. Page 232.

CHAPTER THREE

THE MISSING LINK

During my junior high years, I owned a small dirt bike. It was fast, powerful, loud — and broke down all the time. On one occasion, I had to replace the shattered piston rings. I detached the cylinder and removed from the piston what was left of the piston rings. The inner cylinder was scratched from the broken rings pressing against it. This complicated matters, requiring the cylinder to be bored out (drilled and finished) to a larger size. Moreover, I had to purchase a bigger piston and rings to fit the wider cylinder. It took a while, but finally I finished the repair.

The big moment of truth arrived as I began to kick-start the engine. Sure enough, it started! Honestly, I was a bit surprised. Pressing in the clutch, I shifted into first gear and took off. Before long, I was in fourth gear and tearing up the path at forty miles per hour. Then, without warning, the engine seized, the back tire locked, and the bike skidded to a dead stop.

After all that time, expense, and work, the bike was in far worse shape than when I began. The engine seized, and ground to a halt because I had missed one crucial step in the repair. I had failed to take apart and clean the crankcase below the cylinder. I was unaware that pieces of the old piston rings had fallen into the crankcase. When the repaired engine was started, the metal fragments were flushed back up between the cylinder and the piston — eventually freezing the piston in place.

Like my old dirt bike, our present efforts in adolescent catechesis stand broken and in need of repair. The fact that we have a problem is little contested. What to do about it — well that's another story. Like my initial bike repair, we may quickly focus on what seems obvious on the surface. We need new programs, updated resources, better use of technology, etc. Although these repairs need to be made, they will make little difference if we fail to go to the crankcase of faith development, if you will. Our parishes need to rediscover the power and importance of *affiliative faith*. Without a robust expression of affiliative faith in our parishes, our subsequent efforts in adolescent catechesis and faith development will seize up and ultimately fail.

Back to the Parish

One thing we all seem to agree upon is that our present efforts in adolescent catechesis are less than life altering for many of our Catholic teens. The indictment in the National Study on Youth and Religion (NSYR) was as subtle as a jackhammer. Speaking of Catholic teens, Smith and Denton write, "The majority instead tended to be rather religiously and spiritually indifferent, uninformed, and disengaged."[62]

Recent studies have also demonstrated that life-impacting catechesis and vibrant teen faith are characteristically associated with life-impacting parishes and vibrant congregations. The Exemplary Youth Ministry (EYM) research makes clear that parishes not only matter, but, along with parental influence, are at the heart of adolescent faith formation. The whole congregation needs to reach out to young people.

Affiliative Faith

Before we go any farther, we need to stop and ask what is affliative faith? Understanding this concept is critical for understanding where we must go in reaching today's youth.

The term was coined by John Westerhoff III in his book *Will Our Children Have Faith*. It is both a style or stage in an individual's faith development and a quality of faith reflective of a community's ability to foster a deep sense of belonging. This quality of faith addresses the emotional and relational aspects of faith.

Affiliative faith is an individual style of faith often associated with younger adolescents who have yet to develop their own identity. Before one develops their own sense of self, they borrow and draw strength from the identity of others — those they trust, love, and have their own well-established identities. They borrow beliefs, values, behaviors, etc. from their faith community.

Affiliative faith is also the faith of belonging. A parish that nurtures affiliative faith helps members feel like they are an important part of the community. Affiliative faith socializes people into the practices, values, beliefs, customs, and rituals of the community. Affiliative faith is also the faith of the heart — where one feels the presence of God in the worship, community, and mission of one's faith community.

Parish life plays an incredible role in the formation of young people. When looking at faith formation through the lens of faith development, the connection becomes very clear. Although faith is a gift of God and a work of grace, there is much to learn from faith development theories.

Faith Development

In *Will Our Children Have Faith*, John Westerhoff III introduced a four-style model for faith development (experienced,
affiliative, searching, and owned).[63] Applying this model to
parish life offers insight and helpful tools in fostering the faith
growth, not only in teens, but also in all church members.
Westerhoff likens faith growth to tree development. Like a
tree, faith develops in a gradual way, one ring at a time, and
growth is contingent upon a supportive and nurturing environment. This nurturing environment is created when the
family and faith community intentionally partner to provide
key elements, like positive and trusting relationships in the
parish community, parents living out their faith, and a clear
sense of belonging within the family and parish. Conversely,
faith development is stunted in a poor environment where
parents aren't invested, going to church feels more like entering a morgue than a welcoming community, and members
are isolated from one another's lives. Growth is always a work
of God (see 1 Corinthians 3:5–9), but parents, family, and the
faith community play an important role in facilitating the
right conditions for growth to occur.

Furthermore, when new rings grow on a tree, the previous rings remain. Likewise, faith develops by adding to (not
replacing) already acquired faith styles and experiences. We
do not outgrow previous faith styles, but continue to build
upon the faith experiences of past stages throughout our lives.

Four Styles of Faith

Moving from the center outward, Westerhoff labels the four
styles of faith as Experienced Faith, Affiliative Faith, Searching Faith, and Owned Faith.

1. Experienced Faith

Everyone, no matter their age, begins with this foundational stage. Westerhoff associates this first style of faith with the preschool and early childhood years. Faith results from interactions with the Christian community (family, church, etc.). Faith is experienced before it is understood. It is primarily transmitted through experiences of trust, love, and acceptance within the environment of faith. Experienced Faith imitates and reacts to the faith actions of others.

Our first experience of faith originates from our parents and other significant adults. Like the exuberant six-year-old child who confidently endorses a Republican presidential candidate because his parents are Republican, so a child will imitate the faith of his parents.

2. Affiliative Faith

This second style is often associated with adolescence. First, it can be described as the faith of belonging, where youth act alongside of others in the community who possess a clear sense of identity. Teens are welcomed by adults, feel accepted, are included in ministry, and are valued for their contribution to the faith community. Second, this style is the faith of the heart, characterized by strong religious affections. Teens (and parents) *want* to be at church. Third, affiliative faith accepts the authority of the community to inspire and judge actions and validate faith. This style of faith is certainly important to the faith development of young people, but it also has to be nourished in adult parishioners. (In later writings, Westerhoff combines experienced and affiliative faith into a pathway to God entitled the "experiential way." Since Westerhoff merges these styles, I will be combining experienced and affiliative faith from this point forward.)

3. Searching Faith

This style of faith is often associated with later adolescence and the developmental process of acquiring one's identity. Searching faith seeks to add the faith of one's head to the existing faith of the heart. This process of transitioning from a noncritical acceptance of the community's faith story to a personal faith story includes necessary doubting, critiquing, wrestling, and questioning the meaning and relevance of one's past understanding of faith. The affirmation and acceptance of one's faith community is critical and an essential anchor during the raging storms of searching faith. The normally compliant teen who informs you as you are walking out the door to Mass that he finds no value in wasting his Sunday morning on a boring ritual is definitely in the throes of searching faith.

4. Owned Faith

Owned faith is the culmination of the conversion process. Building upon the existing faith of the heart and head, owned faith motivates one towards significant behavioral change. As a result of searching faith, beliefs and values are internalized, resulting in changed behaviors and lifestyle choices. Owned faith may arrive suddenly or gradually, dramatically or without fanfare, emotionally or intellectually, but it is always the faith of conversion or an actively changed life. A college student, who regularly serves meals at the local soup kitchen, voluntarily helps at youth ministry events, or serves as a Eucharistic minister, is exhibiting some semblance of owned faith.

Faith Formation and Parish Life

Because each stage of faith is contingent upon the previous style, it is imperative that we develop a rich experience of affiliative faith in order to enhance survival when navigating the stormy seas of searching faith. When parish life provides the opportunity for experienced/affiliative, searching and owned faith, the end product is discipleship, which is why providing the soil for faith formation is so important. If our parishes do not offer a deep and sustaining affiliative faith, the resulting lack of belonging or acceptance is so destructive that it becomes the very impetus for teens (and adults) to search in an opposing direction. However, this was not always the case.

Experiencing a strong sense of affiliation, or belonging, was more the norm among Catholic parish members fifty plus years ago. The cultural dynamics at the time rendered the Church both essential and central to life. Many ethnic Catholics lived in homogenous Catholic ghettos where a multitude of voices combined to sing one harmonious chorus. With the local parish as the conductor, the chorale included parents, extended family, and Catholic neighbors.[64] This extensive cultural web of mutually supporting institutions, neighborhoods, and relationships became the primary conveyers of Catholic identity. Young people were naturally socialized into their faith.

Over the past fifty years, the monolithic Catholic chorale has virtually eroded into a cultural solo artist, wrestling for the microphone among a multitude of diverse, sometimes shrill, and often contradictory voices. With the diminishing of anti-Catholicism and the shedding of religious minority status, European Catholic immigrants integrated into mainstream American culture. Additionally, many Catholics attained higher education resulting in greater economic prosperity. These social and economic advancements loosened what was previously a white-knuckled grip of dependence upon the Church as an institution and identity-forming community. In new and more mottled environments, Catholics intermarried and interacted more frequently with those of differing faiths and perspectives. Furthermore, television was electronically piped into almost every Catholic household offering an extensive buffet of channels, replete with every cultural cuisine imaginable, endorsing perspectives, beliefs, values, and morals that were often anything but Catholic. Today, most Catholics identify with, are more influenced by, and more deeply belong to the surrounding larger culture than their Catholic faith. Morphing into sacramental providers, many of our parishes have lost the foundational power of affiliative faith.

Intentionally Developing Affiliative Faith

Nevertheless, affiliate faith remains critical. This type of faith develops by making meaningful connections with families by capitalizing on every opportunity as early as possible, such as marriage preparation or baptism. These events in their lives represent critical access points into the faith community. We not only need to make a connection from families to pastoral leaders, but from families to families, and children to children. For instance, baptismal preparation should include intentional community building within any classes or gatherings. Keeping those connections alive by later organizing baby-sitting co-ops, small groups, annual baptismal anniversary celebrations, and activities for their children will contribute significantly towards transforming a parish from being event driven to being community driven.

Affiliative faith is the dominant style of faith for most teens (and many adults). It is also the faith of the heart. Strong emotional connections are made when one experiences the presence of Jesus in the liturgies, religious education gatherings, and in strong relational bonds with people of faith. As children grow into young adults, they begin to search and question whether the borrowed faith of their parents and church will be adopted as their own. A positive experience with something that is borrowed increases the chances that one will later want to own it for themselves. Without a strong parish affiliation, teens are untethered during the searching years and are vulnerable to floating off into the vast frontiers of spiritual space. They may never glance back, or even worse, have a negative experience of church, which becomes the very propulsion that powerfully blasts them in the opposite direction of God and the church.

Nurturing Searching Faith

Unless we do well in developing affiliative faith, we have little chance of moving teens through searching faith and finally to owned faith. However, once young people begin the process of developing their own identities, they transition towards a searching expression of faith. The faith of their hearts, expressed through the love of their parents, attachment to their faith community, and their experience of the presence of God, now needs to make sense in their heads, and become owned faith.

In his encyclical *Catechesi Tradendae*, Pope John Paul II captured the challenge of catechizing adolescents as they search for a faith of their own:

> But often it is also the age of deeper questioning, of anguished or even frustrating searching, of a certain mistrust of others and dangerous introspection, and the age sometimes of the first experiences of setbacks and of disappointments. Catechesis cannot ignore these changeable aspects of this delicate period of life. A catechesis capable of leading the adolescent to reexamine

his or her life and to engage in dialogue, a catechesis
that does not ignore the adolescent's great questions —
self-giving, belief, love and the means of expressing it
constituted by sexuality — such a catechesis can be de-
cisive. (*Catechesi Tradendae* 38)

For some teens, transitioning into a searching faith re-
sembles a pebble gently rippling through a pond. You may
hardly notice. For others, it is as obvious and passionate as
a tsunami smacking the shore. Either way, we do well by
not reacting fearfully, or obstructing honest inquiry or even
belligerent challenges. Too often, we can feel threatened by
tough questions and resort to minimizing, moralizing, or
even shaming teens. In many ways, the manner in which we
handle these questions is as significant as the answers we provide. In some cases, it is more significant.

I've met teens who dismissed the Church because they
felt dismissed by their parish leaders when asking challenging questions or disagreeing with the Church's position. It is
not critical that we possess the ability to answer every question, but it is critical that we demonstrate respect, authentically embrace their questions, and provide a safe, accepting,
and loving environment. We can affirm teens by responding
to tough questions by saying, "Wow, that's a great question. I
wish I were smart enough to answer it off the top of my head!
I'll do some research and see what I can come up with." After the meeting, ask your pastor or other authority, and read,
research, etc. Share what you came up with during the next
meeting. Sometimes your answers won't be satisfying, or you
have no answer but one of paradox. Postmodern teens are
more at ease with messiness and ambiguity. But more than

anything keep respecting, loving, and walking with teens on the sometimes, treacherous journey to owned faith.

Home to Owned Faith

Over the many years in youth ministry, I've witnessed some pretty incredible acts of faith by young people. I watched many of them put their faith on the line and risk their reputations among their peers on account of their deep commitment to live for Jesus. Many were young heroes and heroines among their peers in our parish community. I was truly convinced I was seeing the best of owned teenage faith — until they went away to college. I saw more than a few of these teens for whom I had already begun the beatification process when in high school, begin questioning their faith and experimenting with different lifestyles. What I thought was owned faith was in reality affiliative faith. While in college, they experienced greater intellectual and moral challenges, and they entered the stage of searching faith.

Jeff was one such young man. When I met him during the end of his freshman year in high school, he already had personal faith experiences from some youth conferences he attended.

Jeff had personal faith experiences, parents who lived the faith, a family that was deeply involved in the parish community, participated in the youth ministry, and exercised leadership. I also sensed he had a call on his life. I thought he was a fine example of owned teenage faith — until twelfth grade. During Jeff's senior year, he started dating, trying on new peer groups, and questioning his faith. When he left for college, he drifted away further. He became proficient in behaviors and activities that only a few years earlier he despised. During his senior year, he experienced a whole new level of emptiness, and he drew upon spiritual memories, his parent's faith, and meaningful relationships that reflected a happier, more peaceful time in his life. Jeff was tethered to a deep and meaningful affiliative faith. The faith borrowed during his teen years was left behind while searching in college, but eventually became his own during his early twenties. His journey illustrates how faith can develop when each of the faith styles are nurtured well. Oh, and yes, he did have a call to ministry. Today, he is one of the absolute best parish pastoral ministers I know.

FOR CONSIDERATION

- What is the hidden curriculum of your parish — the curriculum never taught, but thoroughly formed in the hearts and minds of young people through the parish culture?

  What unspoken message is the parish really sending to all who come on Sunday?
- Consider your own faith journey in light of Westerhoff's styles of faith.
- How would you generally rate your parish's ability to nurture affiliative faith in young people?
- In what ways is your parish making connections with families when their children are young? How are these connections built upon over the years?
- If affiliative faith is "borrowed faith," are teens borrowing the kind of faith experience from the parish community that they would later want to make their own? Please explain your answer.
- In what practical ways can catechists or youth ministers demonstrate respect, authentically embrace teens' questions, and provide a safe, accepting, and loving environment for honest inquiry?

Notes

62. *Soul Searching: The Religious and Spiritual Lives of American Teenagers.* Christian Smith with Melinda Lundquist Denton. Oxford University Press, 2005. Page 195.

63. John Westerhoff III, *Will Our Children Have Faith?* Seabury Press, 1976. In later writings, Westerhoff moves from a tree to a pilgrimage metaphor and combines Experienced and Affiliative faith into a pathway to God entitled the "experiential way." John Westerhoff III, *Will Our Children Have Faith? Revised Edition.* Morehouse Publishing, 2000. Page 101.

64. This remains the case for many first- and second-generation Latino youth. They spend more time with their families and intergenerational communities who live in close proximity. These tight networks reinforce their faith, customs, values, etc. Third-generation Latino teens more resemble white youth in the time they spend with their peers and their isolation from family. The result is greater vulnerability to risky behaviors. See *Growing Up in America, The Power of Race in the Lives of Teens.* Brad Christerson, Korie L. Edwards, and Richard Flory. Stanford University Press, 2010.

CHAPTER FOUR

THE YOUTH-ENGAGING PARISH

"Can you repeat that?" I was certain I lost something while decoding a Texan drawl.

Kurt, a youth minister I had just met, patiently restated, "Fourteen young men from my parish are in various stages of seminary."

I was stunned, thinking, "Maybe a total of fourteen young men studying for the priesthood from across the diocese ... or, maybe fourteen seminarians throughout a 100-year parish history ... but fourteen at one time from a single parish? That's unheard-of! What kind of parish does that?"

Several months later, I spent a few days at Kurt's parish. Afterwards, his story didn't strike me as so implausible. Listening to several teen and parent groups, I discovered something special, almost palpable: a culture that not only supported and encouraged a call to the priesthood, but more importantly, an environment that formed disciples across generations. Both young and old spoke of an environment where they experienced a strong sense of belonging, a meaningful connection with others, the personal care of parish leaders, and a community where their faith was intentionally fostered.

Members of St. Anne were not simply attending and liking church — they were deeply connected and gripped by the experience. It was apparent to me that both parents and teens shared a strong emotional attachment to their parish, and felt deeply rooted in their faith and in the life of the community. The parish offered life and vitality that spiritually nourished and sustained adults and teens alike. It begs the question: What are they doing right?

Mature Teenage Disciples

All of St. Anne's activities, programs, events, and relationships are concentrated into a single focus: discipleship. Bottom line, exemplary parish youth ministry is all about making disciples of Jesus Christ. But with that said, what does teenage discipleship look like? What are the telltale signs of a mature Christian disciple? Over the years, several research studies[65] have addressed this question and carefully developed specific criteria or "end products." The following seven categories broadly summarize what a maturing Christian teen looks like.[66]

1. They Actively Pursue Spiritual Growth

Both alone and in the company of others, they pursue spiritual growth through conversations, study, reading the Bible, prayer, small groups, retreats, and other spiritual activities. They participate in gatherings where they can ask sincere questions, grow in an understanding of their faith, learn to speak more intelligently about it, and have an opportunity to build strong friendships.

2. They Are Aware of God's Presence

These teens can quickly and clearly answer the question, "What's God doing in your life?" They experience everyday life through the eyes of faith. They see God's presence and activity in their own lives, the lives of others, and in the world around them. They are known to seek and experience God's guidance, are aware of God's work in their lives, and show confidence in God working for the good, even in difficult matters.

3. They Actively Live Their Faith

These teens are not "secret agents" for Jesus — working in the shadows, inaudibly executing covert, heavenly operations. Instead, they actively respond to God's call in their lives, fusing their faith into everyday conversations, choices, and behaviors.

4. They Are Active in the Faith in Community

These teens are not operating under the banner "spiritual but not religious." They are active in their communities of faith, regularly attending worship gatherings, involved in teaching, service, fund-raising, and church committees. They actively embrace stewardship, giving of their time, talent, and even treasure.

5. They Have a Hopeful and Positive Disposition

These teenagers reflect a joyful, positive, and hopeful attitude towards life and others. They enjoy being with people, including those with diverse backgrounds and views, and show graciousness with those who are different or shunned by others. They exhibit optimism, cooperation, and belief in others and have the conviction that one person can make a difference.

6. They Are Active in Service

On a personal and organizational level, these teens care about others by serving their church, surrounding community, and larger world. They reach out and support those in need, study about and want to impact issues of injustice and immorality.

7. They Live with Christian Integrity

Not simply talking the walk, but walking the talk, the young person with mature Christian faith uses the Scriptures as a guide for discerning right and wrong. They enjoy positive reputations for honesty, care about others, exhibit classroom integrity, and live drug and alcohol free lives.

If you're anything like me, the first time I read over the characteristics of "maturing Christian youth," I mused to myself, "Who produces these kinds of teens?" To be totally honest, I wondered what parish churns out *adults* resembling this profile.

In 2004, a Lily-funded research project entitled *The Study of Exemplary Congregations in Youth Ministry* (EYM) attempted to answer these questions. Maybe one of the best kept secrets in youth ministry, the purpose of the EYM study was "to identify congregations that consistently establish faith as a vital factor in the lives of their youth and young adults, to discover what accounts for their effective approach to ministry, and to make the results widely available for the benefit of other congregations."[67]

The ecumenical project utilized both quantitative and qualitative research methods[68] while studying 131 congregations that consistently produced teens of mature Christian faith. Twenty-one congregations from seven denominations[69] were studied on site and in greater depth (a small-, medium-, and large-sized assembly[70] from each of the seven denominations, representing all regions of the United States). The EYM research uncovered some "eye-opening" commonalities among these exemplary ministries with youth.

Spirit and Culture of Youth Ministry

The EYM study found that the robust expression of teenage faith produced by exemplary congregations was a result of *the culture or spirit of the whole church:*

> The EYM study discovered that it is the culture of the whole church that is most influential in nurturing youth of vital Christian faith. The genius of these churches seems best described as a systemic mix of theology, values, people, relationships, expectations, and activities. It appears that a culture of the Spirit emerges with its pervasive and distinct dynamics and atmosphere that is more powerful than its component parts.[71]

Before examining some of the common ingredients of a congregational culture that consistently produces teenage disciples, it's essential to note that the EYM research makes it clear that we must recalibrate our understanding of the nature of youth ministry. We must, once and for all, definitively give up on the idea that a thriving youth ministry can spring up in isolation from the larger parish. An isolated youth group, marooned from adult members, meeting in a semi-remodeled church bomb shelter/youth room, and led by a couple of charismatic adults is simply not enough to produce a concentrated, potent form of teenage discipleship in today's culture.

On a foundational level, the study reveals that exemplary churches, although denominationally diverse, share similar theological contours that profoundly shape their congregational identities. Like a compass, core theological beliefs regarding the nature and workings of God, direct energy and conviction towards every value, commitment, and practice.

Three Generations of Youth Ministry

Modern Catholic youth ministry has evolved in many ways over the past forty years.[72] Responding to changing conditions, needs, and contexts of teens, the American Church has progressed through three general parish expressions or generations of youth ministry. Like software, not every parish upgrades their approach with each new release. Therefore, you will find expressions of each version in parishes today.

1. The Youth Group (YM 1.0)

A common expression of parish teen ministry that emerged after the societal changes of the late sixties and early seventies was often generically referred to as "the youth group."[73] These gatherings were often one dimensional, focusing upon a social, spiritual, athletic, or service component of ministry. Participants tended to be somewhat of a homogenous crowd, often becoming their own social group or even clique. In many ways, the "youth group" was not yet a "youth ministry." Most lacked a unifying set of goals and a comprehensive and integrated approach to youth ministry. Commonly led by a charismatic priest or volunteer adult or couple, youth groups often experienced sudden starts and stops. When the leader was transferred, moved-on, or burned out, the youth group often adjourned with them.

2. Comprehensive Youth Ministry (YM 2.0)

In 1976, the U.S.C.C. Department of Education published a landmark document entitled *A Vision of Youth Ministry*,[74] giving birth to "comprehensive youth ministry." This second generation of Catholic youth ministry provided a framework for comprehensive ministry to, by, for, and with teens. Furthermore, it articulated a clear focus expressed through two central goals:

1. Youth ministry works to foster the total personal and spiritual growth of each young person.

2. Youth ministry seeks to draw young people to responsible participation in the life, mission and work of the faith community.[75]

In addition, the *Vision* offered a pastorally balanced and integrated approach to youth ministry through the expression of seven components of youth ministry: Word, (evangelization and catechesis), Worship, Creating Community, Guidance and Healing, Justice and Service, Enablement, and Advocacy. Other key developments included moving beyond a homogenous audience to a multifaceted approach addressing the various spiritual dispositions of teens. Furthermore, the *Vision* moved youth ministry beyond the guru youth minister to a "youth ministry coordinator" and a team-based approach. Instead of one person or couple leading a group, the leadership expanded to involve many members of the community offering their gifts, talents, and time towards various coordinated ministries.

3. Third-Generation Catholic Youth Ministry (YM 3.0)

A third generation of Catholic youth ministry saw its beginnings in the late 90s with the publication of the U.S. Bishops pastoral plan for youth ministry, entitled *Renewing the Vision — A Framework for Catholic Youth Ministry.*[76] Building upon the past foundation of *A Vision of Youth Ministry,* and responding to the present changes in contemporary society, *Renewing the Vision* took Catholic youth ministry in several fresh directions.

First, it recognized the eagerness of present-day teens to be fully involved as the "church of today" by adding a third

Continued on next page

goal to the previous two: To empower young people to live as disciples of Jesus Christ in our world today.

Second, *Renewing the Vision,* along with the research findings of the National Study on Youth and Religion, reaffirmed the importance of the family as the primary context for faith development. The result is an increased emphasis on intergenerational ministry and ministry to parents and families.

Third, the research concludes:

> *Renewing the Vision* focused attention on the power of community — the church community, the family community, and the wider community — for promoting healthy adolescent development and faith growth. *Renewing the Vision* re-affirmed the truth that youth ministry is the work of the entire Church and that youth ministry is to draw upon the faith, the gifts, the talents, the energies, and the resources of the entire church community.[77]

"Third-generation youth ministry" expands the boundaries to a macrolevel parish approach. In other words, the effectiveness of a youth ministry is intimately connected to the health, vitality, leadership, and vision of the larger faith community. The parish community — with its relationships, values, theology, mission, practices, and activities — acts as a life- and faith- shaping system for teens. Furthermore, ministry with teens is not the exclusive responsibility of the youth ministry coordinator and team. Rather, the entire faith community and their embodied expression of intergenerational discipleship is the primary delivery system.

At their very core, these exemplary congregations specifically emphasize discipleship, prayer, Scripture, and mission. Everyone, exclusive of age, is called to personally know and follow Jesus as a disciple. Prayer and Scripture, recognized and valued as living sources of God's presence, direction, and transforming power, are utilized both individually and corporately. Living the faith and participating in the mission of the church through witnessing, serving, and promoting justice and moral responsibility are embraced and understood to be central to one's life. Furthermore, vitality of faith can be traced to a theological conviction that God is experientially present in all of life. These congregations perceive Jesus' living and active presence embodied in worship, study, service, and in one another as community.

Shaped and flowing from these theological convictions, the EYM churches reveal common strategic commitments. Because God is real, present, and actively working in their communities (in actual fact they understand themselves to be the "Body of Christ") they seek to strategically live out Jesus' mission in the world. These congregations intentionally emphasize and strategically organize their efforts towards reaching out, forming disciples, and serving others. In many ways, the life-pumping heart of these churches is their theological conviction that God is alive and present in their communities. This life is then imparted to others via the arteries and veins of their congregation's strategic commitments.

Intersecting Spheres of Ministry

The genius and power of EYM congregations resides in multiple, intersecting spheres of influence on the youth of their churches. Combined together, they form a life-impacting culture. These spheres of ministry include the larger congregation, age-level ministries, household ministry, and congregational leadership.

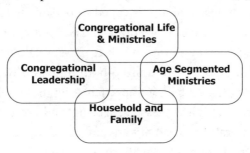

1. The Larger Congregation

Instead of being viewed as the "future church," young people are warmly welcomed on every level as the "present church." Young people are expected to participate, discover and use their gifts, make decisions, and lead larger church activities. At their very core, EYM congregations are intergenerational.

Furthermore, young people benefit from the rich vitality that characterizes the relationships, values, expectations, and practices of the larger church. EYM congregations value people, especially youth, by providing a safe and hospitable environment. Thoroughly included, teens enjoy quality relationships and meaningful support from intergenerational groups. These congregations are committed to excellence, welcome new ideas, and encourage questioning and thinking from young members. As an integral part of their larger church experience, teenagers are challenged to live in a morally responsible manner and given congregational opportunities to serve.

2. Age-Level Ministry

EYM congregations also offer a variety of well-organized, planned, innovative, and contextualized age-level ministries for teens. Many of the churches attribute their particular effectiveness to a strong evangelical emphasis. Focusing on the person of Jesus Christ, these youth ministries major on helping teens know, love, and serve Jesus as teenage disciples. Rather than supplying exhaustive answers to the questions teens aren't really asking, EYM teen ministries address a broad range of real teen issues. Finally, teens feel welcomed, accepted, and supported through a web of meaningful peer-to-peer or adult-to-peer relationships.

3. Household Family Ministry

The National Study on Youth and Religion made one finding crystal clear to those who work with teens: "The best way to get most youth involved in and serious about their faith communities is to get their parents more involved in and serious about their faith communities."[78] The EYM study confirms the NSYR findings. Exemplary congregations emphasize the same message of discipleship with the parents of teens resulting in many parents living a vital and committed faith. Their children, in turn, tend to look spiritually similar. EYM churches educate parents in their own faith and equip parents in nurturing the faith of their children. These congregations promote and support household practices such as family prayer, faith discussions, bible reading, and service. They also offer programs and events focusing on strengthening parent and teen relationships.

4. Congregational Leadership

Trained, competent, and caring leaders on every level positively impact the young people of EYM churches, beginning with the pastor.

The pastor plays a critical and powerful role in these exemplary congregations. Pastors influence young people in three specific ways. First, their spiritual influence is felt as they authentically share and live their personal faith. Pastors who exercise personal integrity, honesty, vulnerability, and a prayerful dependence upon God provide a concrete illustration of faith maturity and powerfully touch the lives of teens. Second, the pastor interpersonally connects with teens. Young people from EYM congregations feel their pastors communicate clearly, genuinely listen to others, treat church members as family, and build a strong sense of parish community. Third, the pastor supports the youth ministry and the adult and teen leaders of the youth ministry. Although the pastor need not be involved in all the details of the youth ministry, it is essential that he actively and enthusiastically supports and advocates for it. EYM congregation pastors appreciate, value, and trust the youth minister and adult youth ministry team.

The next sphere of influence comes from youth ministers. Young people of EYM churches benefit greatly from the exceptional leadership of their youth ministers. The leaders model, live, and effectively mentor adults and teens in the faith. They know the faith, teens, and youth culture. Sharing a clear vision, they attract and equip a team of adult and teen leaders. They maintain positive and life-impacting relationships with teens, parents, adult leaders, and church staff.

Finally, adult and teen leaders effectively model spiritual vitality. Leaders foster genuine relationships with teens, operate out of a clear sense of vision, and effectively mentor teens in the faith.

In the end, EYM congregations powerfully impact the teens of their churches as a result of the overlapping partnerships with the larger congregation, age-segmented youth ministries, family ministries, and congregational leadership.

Clear and Worthy Destination

If we hope to truly reach a new generation of teens, we must begin with a clear and worthy destination. Without a spiritual destination firmly embedded in our minds, we may have no real idea where we're heading, get lost on the way, and finally end up going through the programmatic motions of religious education, or Confirmation preparation, which can easily take on a life of their own. We end up measuring success by simply getting through another year, and we've actually gone nowhere. This cycle can repeat itself for years on end.

In addition, if the destination we have in mind is nothing more than a spiritual bunny hill, teens will quickly leave it behind in search of more challenging slopes. In our attempt to make the gospel more attractive by leaving out the core message of discipleship, we can inadvertently make it less appealing to young people today.

Likewise, a ministry with teens driven by anything less than giving one's all, will eventually end up on the sidelines of their lives. By domesticating the gospel we strip it of its dignity, power, and ultimately its appeal. A faith not worth dying for, in the end, is not worth living for either. Our ministry with young people must have a destination worthy of their lives. That destination is discipleship.

The value and subsequent appeal of the EYM study is that it begins and ends with discipleship. The success of these churches has everything to do with their high expectations. While many churches under-challenge teens towards inactivity, EYM congregations inspire teens to discover a worthy adventure in which to invest their lives.

Faith Assets

The EYM research identified 44 Faith Assets, specific characteristics or building blocks of the culture of EYM churches. Although not heralded as "the definitive list," but a growing body of knowledge, these Faith Assets provide a helpful roadmap for nurturing the kind of congregational culture that consistently grows maturing teen disciples.

The Faith Assets are divided into following four sections, or spheres of ministry: 1) Congregational Faith and Qualities; 2) Age-Level Ministries; 3) Family and Household Faith; 4) Leadership. (Appendix A includes a full description of all 44 Faith Assets along with a practical assessment tool.)

1. Congregational Faith and Qualities

The first eighteen assets describe Congregational Faith and Qualities. These dimensions of ministry depict the theological emphasis, strategic focus, and the qualities of community life in the larger parish that impact teens.

2. Age-Level Ministries

The second group of Faith Assets describes the qualities of the youth ministry. Six assets detail the values, expectations, and practices of the teen ministries.

3. Family and Household Faith

The third grouping of Faith Assets describes the overlapping influence of family life on youth. Five Faith Assets relate household faith and practices, and the congregational support of parents and families.

4. Leadership

The final cluster of Faith Assets describe the qualities and competencies of church leadership on several levels, including the pastor, youth minister, adult leadership team, and teens.

FOR CONSIDERATION

- What is the overall focus of your parish? To what extent is the call to discipleship a priority of your parish?

- How would you rate the efforts of your parish in regard to the seven broad categories of Christian maturity? In which area do you feel you are doing best? What area needs the most improvement? What are some practical steps you might take in order to be more effective?

- From what generation of youth ministry does your parish primarily operate? What steps would need to be taken in order to improve where you are and/or move to the next generation?

- What is the mission statement of your parish? What is the significance to you knowing it or not knowing it? How does it guide your parish?

- On a 1 to 10 scale (1 being low and 10 being high), how would you rate the level of youth-friendliness and inclusion of teens in the overall life of the parish? In what ways can teens be made more welcome? In what ministries might teens be invited to greater involvement?

Notes

65. The seven characteristics referenced were primarily taken from the Exemplary Youth Ministry Study.

66. *The Spirit and Culture of Youth Ministry, Leading Congregations toward Exemplary Youth Ministry*. Roland Martinson, Wes Black, John Roberto. EYM Publishing, 2010. This is a must-read youth ministry resource.

67. Quoted from The Spirit of Youth Ministry, National Conference binder, Session One: Research Project Overview, page 2, John Roberto, *The Spirit of Youth Ministry*. Center for Ministry Development, ©2006. Available as a Journal article on www.YouthMinistryAccess.org.

68. Surveys ranged from 301-354 questions of their pastor, primary youth leader, volunteers, parents, and youth. A total of 5,796 individuals (2,252 young people) were surveyed. Additionally, 222 pastors and youth ministers from the 131 congregations provided responses to four open-ended questions regarding their youth ministries. The 21 site visits included in-depth interviews with staff and members of each congregation. (The Spirit of Youth Ministry, National Conference binder, Session One: Research Project Overview, page 2.)

69. The seven denominations included Assemblies of God, Evangelical Covenant, Evangelical Lutheran Church of America (ELCA), Presbyterian Church USA, Roman Catholic, Southern Baptist, and United Methodist Church.

70. Small congregation: fewer than 250 in weekly worship attendance; Medium congregation: 251-750 in weekly worship attendance; Large congregation: more than 751 in weekly worship attendance.

71. *The Spirit and Culture of Youth Ministry, Leading Congregations Toward Exemplary Youth Ministry*. Roland Martinson, Wes Black, John Roberto. EYM Publishing, 2010. Quoted from page 50.

72. For a more precise and detailed history see *Leadership in Youth Ministry*, Center for Ministry Development, Chapter 1, History of Youth Ministry, John Roberto.

73. Technically, before YM 1.0 there were CYO clubs/groups in the 1950s. They were the first youth group.

74. United States Catholic Conference Department of Education. *A Vision of Youth Ministry*. Washington, DC: USCC Office of Publishing, 1976.

75. *A Vision of Youth Ministry* 7.

76. United States Conference of Catholic Bishops. Renewing the Vision — A Framework for Catholic Youth Ministry. Washington, DC: Office of Publishing, 1997.

77. Quoted from: *Leadership in Youth Ministry*. Center for Ministry Development Staff. Twenty-third Publications, New London: 2009. Chapter Two, History of Youth Ministry, John Roberto.

78. Christian Smith with Melinda Lundquist Denton. *Soul Searching: The Religious and Spiritual Lives of Teenagers* (New York: Oxford University Press, 2005), page 57.

CHAPTER FIVE

FROM EVANGELIZING
TO IMMANUELIZING

Maybe the best-kept secret of being Catholic is that evangelization stands front and center to Catholicism. The commission to share our faith arrives via our baptism. The Scriptures trumpet the mandate to proclaim the gospel to all nations.[79] Pope Paul VI established the legitimacy and even primacy of evangelization in modern times by asserting that the "[Church] exists to evangelize" and "evangelization is the essential mission of the Church."[80] Pope John Paul II frequently challenged the Church to reach a contemporary world by practicing a "new evangelization."

Over the years, the word "evangelization" has acquired some fairly negative connotations among Catholics and society as a whole. What originally and literally meant "a messenger of good news" frequently telegraphs feelings of "bad news" among people today. The Greek noun *euangelion* was used in a secular sense to describe a herald announcing good news, such as a wedding or an important military victory. The New Testament uses the word to describe the messenger and content of the good news of God's Kingdom through Jesus Christ. However, when personally encountering well-intentioned but overzealous Christians whose main goal is to add one more number to their ticker of souls saved, many Catholics felt like evangelistic prey. Not surprisingly, these experiences did not help launch the ministry of evangelization into the mainstream of Catholicism. Let's just say that most Catholics felt that bingo was more Catholic than evangelization. [81]

Evangelization is supposed to be the sharing of the good news of God's loving invitation to all people to become citizens of God's kingdom of peace — made possible by Jesus' suffering, death, and resurrection. This message of the Kingdom fills the vacuum of our souls by addressing our insatiable hunger for peace — peace with God, peace with one another, and peace within ourselves. Furthermore, when the message of the Kingdom embodies the systems, values, and priorities of an entire culture (in the form of social justice), the result is a transformed nation or world. The U.S. Bishops say, "The fruit of evangelization is changed lives and a changed world — holiness and justice, spirituality and peace."[82]

It must be reasoned that if evangelization is the essential mission of the Church, then it must be the essential mission of youth ministry. In other words, evangelization — inviting young people into a life-changing relationship with Jesus and the Catholic community — should be at the heart and center of all Catholic youth ministry. Generally speaking, evangelization is the precursor to discipleship.

Surveying the Landscape

According to The Pew U.S. Religious Landscape Survey, the Catholic share of the U.S. adult population has held steady at 25 percent over the past decades. "What this apparent stability obscures, however, is the large number of people who have left the Catholic Church. Approximately one-third of the survey respondents who say they were raised Catholic no longer describe themselves as Catholic. This means that roughly 10 percent of all Americans are former Catholics. These losses, however, have been partly offset by the number of people who have changed their affiliation to Catholicism (2.6 percent of the adult population) but more importantly by the disproportionately high number of Catholics among immigrants to the U.S. The result is that the overall percentage of the population that identifies as Catholic has remained fairly stable."[83] In the end, the Catholic Church records a net loss of 7.5 percent when comparing childhood affiliation to current affiliation. That figure was by far the largest loss of any denomination.[84] The largest net gainers in the survey were those who identify themselves as "unaffiliated." That group rose 8.8 percent.[85] Over one in four (27 perccent) of those who currently identify themselves as "unaffiliated" were once Catholic.[86]

If that weren't bleak enough, although the Scriptures and Church documents point to the primacy of evangelization, and we've made significant practical progress through various renewal efforts,[87] evangelization has yet to fully enter the spiritual bloodstream of the average Catholic. We remain under the shadow of our history, where religious professionals took on the bulk of missionary activities. Though many in religious life sacrifice their very lives to reach others with the good news, most Catholics in the pews do not yet commonly share both the value and practice of evangelization as an essential expression of what it means to live out their Catholic faith.

Indeed if evangelization is about sharing good news, our recent evangelistic efforts appear to be anything but good news. According to The Official Catholic Directory, in 2009, Catholics had the lowest number of adults joining the Church in the previous ten years. Compared to 2001, the number declined 30 percent.[88] If Mass attendance is indicative of our effectiveness, things don't look any better. The percentage of Catholics attending Mass weekly has progressively plunged southward over the past sixty years. In 1945, 75 percent of adult Catholics in the United States attended Mass weekly. In 1965 it dropped to 70 percent; in 1985, 53 percent; in 1995, 43 percent; and down to 34 percent in 2005.[89] More recently, a Center for the Applied Research in the Apostolate (CARA) study reported the number of adults attending Mass weekly plummeted to 23 percent in 2008.[90] Furthermore, 56 percent of adult Catholics rarely or never attend Mass or attend a few times a year.[91]

These statistics leave one wondering, "Where have all the Catholics gone? Are they participating in other denominations or not attending Church at all?"

Millennial Generation

The evangelistic forecast doesn't appear brighter when scanning the next generation on the horizon. Trends among Millennial Generation young adults point towards further decline. According to Pew's report *Religion Among the Millennials*,[92] only 18% of Millennial Generation young adults (18–29 years old) attend church weekly or almost weekly. That is the lowest rate of any previous generation during that period in their lives. Furthermore, 26% of Millennial young adults are religiously unaffiliated. Based upon current trends, David T. Olsen predicts that overall U.S. church attendance will drop to 14.7 percent by 2020.[93]

Finally, most teenagers' Mass attendance closely tracks their parents' attendance practices. Perhaps their post-Confirmation involvement in parish ministry, religious education, or youth ministry serves as a more accurate barometer of their future faith commitment. For most parishes, the vast majority of young people drop out of religious education once confirmed. By the time teens reach their senior year in high school, very few remain involved in anything. Furthermore, most parish youth

Public Relations Crisis

Christianity in general suffers a serious public relations crisis, especially among young people. In 2006, Barna Research reported that 38% of 16- to 29-year-olds outside the church have "a bad impression of present-day Christianity."[94] Furthermore, "hypocrisy" has evolved into a virtual synonym for "Christian" among young people. Barna research reports that 85% of those outside of Christianity who have had sufficient exposure to Christians and churches felt the statement "hypocritical — saying one thing, doing another'" accurately described present-day Christianity.[95] Along with hypocrisy, judgmental (87%) and anti-homosexual (91%) round out the top three most common perceptions of present-day Christianity.[96] If Catholics are uncomfortable with evangelization, society as a whole has become immune to our message and "example" over the past thirty years.

We may reason that outsiders have always been critical of Christianity. Yet, a new, disturbing and rising "inside" demographic has emerged — Christians abandoning the church not because they lost their faith, but, ironically, in order to save their faith. They contend that the church is more an enemy than ally while attempting to follow Jesus. Plagued by scandal, infighting, and yoking with political parties, some contend there is little resemblance between the institutional church and Jesus.[97] In the end, the Church seems to be suffering from a major disconnection with both those inside and outside her walls.

ministries attract only a small fraction of registered teens, let alone religiously unaffiliated youth in the community.

Granted, the decline in church attendance may make headlines, but the southward slide may not necessarily tell the entire story. Going to Mass regularly is not entirely synonymous with evangelistic success. An increasing number of Catholics believe they can be a good Catholic without going to Mass every Sunday.[98] This isn't good news. How deeply can one be evangelized when ignoring a central teaching of the Catholic faith? The National Study on Youth and Religion issued an alarming indictment on the state of Catholic adolescents and concluded that it was only reflective of their parents' faith commitments. Declining church attendance may not tell the entire evangelistic story, but it is reflective of entire southward direction of Catholics practicing their faith.

Facing the Times

My wife Diane and I have a dual heating control electric blanket. One winter night, I woke up feeling chilled. I turned up my side. I heard Diane complaining that she was feeling warm and turned her control down. Still feeling cold, I raised my control up another notch. I heard Diane on the other side of the bed sighing and reaching for her controls. As the night wore on, I was freezing and cranked the control to the highest setting. By morning my teeth were chattering! I looked across the bed at my wife and she had the blanket stripped off with only a sheet on top of her!

Suspicious, we follow the cords, and sure enough, our controls were switched. Every time we tried to remedy our situation with what worked reliably in the past, it had an opposite effect! In a similar manner, the cultural controls of our world have switched with many of us unaware. Maintaining business as usual or simply tinkering with the approaches and methodologies that have brought us to this point only increases the odds that our church attendance will continue to slide in a southward direction.

Rodney Clapp identifies *sentimental capitulation*[99] as one response of the church when facing this situation. Basically, the church acquiesces to the surrounding culture that she has nothing distinctive or robust to offer and capitulates to only providing perfunctory religious ceremonies with which people still have some sentimental attachment. In other words, the Church functions on the fringes of society, interacting as a sacramental dispenser in people's lives.

A second response is to reclaim the past. It's almost instinctual to turn backwards during times of instability. When losing our footing we may flail frantically, clinging to the security and comfort of the steady ground of the past. We may even canonize our fears, concealing them in a rally cry — condemning the present times and summoning people back to the glory days of old. Often, the greatest resistance to the present move of the Spirit comes from the innovators and implementers of the last move of the Spirit. Turning the ship backwards, although offering a sense of security and solidarity in unstable times, in the end, only petrifies our irrelevancy. We have to do more than place our churches on artificial respiration. We have to live in, respond to, and bring real life into the times we find ourselves in — not retreat towards the times in which we would rather live and condemn those who don't want to live them with us.

An Emerging Spirituality

As much as the Church's current crisis constitutes a danger, it equally brims with opportunity. It's during moments like these — when dark clouds overshadow our hopes, that God's power has the most potential to break through. The darkness of failure always precedes the dawning of dependence, which results in the bright midday of God's movement.

The struggle to reach a changing world is a reoccurring theme throughout the Church's history. In his book *Transforming Mission*, David Bosch demonstrates how the theology of mission was defined and redefined with every paradigmatic shift over history.[100] Quoting Hendrik Kraemer, he writes, "Strictly speaking, one ought to always say the Church is in a state of crisis and that its greatest shortcoming is that it is only occasionally aware of it ... [the church] has always needed apparent failure and suffering in order to become fully alive to its real nature and mission."[101]

So where is all this taking us? Can our apparent failure to attract and engage Catholic adults and youth lead to a new beginning? I believe it can if we are willing to be humble and painfully honest. As twenty-first-century Catholics, we are far from the level of Olympic evangelizers. But just when we were shedding the terror associated with the word "evangelize" and removing our training wheels, the cultural terrain changed. We've lost our balance again with the arrival of postmodern young people and the score of parents who travel the same epistemological path. Not only have times changed, but also people have changed, and if we are going to reach this generation as a Church, we must change.

The reality is — evangelization doesn't work any longer. That is, the way we have been doing it during the modern era doesn't work. We need a fresh approach that addresses the spiritual hungers of a postmodern people, but we need to be clear on one thing: Jesus remains the foundation of the Church's mission. Christianity is Jesus. His life addresses the hunger of all humanity in all times. How we understand or experience those hungers is often dependent upon the historical and cultural context in which we live. Understanding the spiritual pangs of our times is critical to the effectiveness of our mission.

A new spirituality is emerging as we increasingly view our world through a postmodern lens. In their book, *Finding Faith*, Richard Flory and Donald E. Miller describe this emerging spirituality among Post Boomers as "expressive communalism."[102]

Expressive Communalism places an emphasis upon embodiment and community. People desire a deep, personal faith experience within the context of a close-knit and meaningful physical community. There is a hunger to belong, serve within the community, and serve others through social outreach outside the community. Moving away from a strictly rational faith, many Post Boomers hunger for a more holistic expression of faith that makes cognitive sense, but is more an embodied experience through worship, teaching, and concrete forms of service. Valuing organic grassroots leadership, they respond well to a participative style.

Addressing the contours of this emerging spirituality requires a retooling of our modern forms of evangelization. The times necessitate that we move from evangelizing to *immanuelizing*.

Immanuelization

First, let's be clear — I am not in any way suggesting that we retire the word evangelization from our ecclesial vocabulary! (God knows I don't have that kind of authority!) The call to evangelize remains in full force and will until the end of time. What I am suggesting is that we upgrade our evangelistic approaches in order to be more compatible with the newer postmodern operating system that young people have adopted as their epistemological platform.

In reality, immanuelization is only a twenty-first-century expression of evangelization. Framing a new evangelization around the concept of the "Immanuel" (God with us) is critical because it fundamentally roots its expression in the theology of incarnation. The incarnation is so profound and radical that it becomes the primary impulse for all God's working in the world. As it defines Jesus' mission, so it gives shape to the church's continuation of that mission today. So what is immanuelization?

Being God's presence

Isaiah provided a prophetic description of Jesus some 700 years before his birth. "Therefore the Lord will give you a sign: The virgin will be with child and give birth to a son, and will call him Immanuel" (Isaiah 7:14). The Gospel of Matthew not only connects the prophecy to Jesus' birth but also discloses the meaning of the name. Immanuel means "God with us" (Matthew 1:22–23). Jesus was God with us — the very presence of God on earth. Being near Jesus meant quite literally you were in the presence of God. Similarly, if we hope to reach the present generation, we, too, must "immanuelize" by being God's presence in our world.

There is nothing novel or original to this call. The Apostle Paul described the church as the Body of Christ (1 Corinthians 12:27). In other words, once Jesus ascended into heaven, we are called and expected to be the very real presence of Jesus in our world. Modern, rational thought hijacked this reality, leaving behind an anemic, disembodied understanding of it.

Modernity led by abstraction. Postmodernity leads by concretizing. To incarnate actually means to make something concrete and real. The word literally means embodied in flesh or taking on flesh. Because postmodern truth arrives through the world of experience, the church must communicate the gospel experientially. In other words, we must operate as the embodied and experiential presence of Jesus. We can't just talk about God's love; we've got to *be* God's love. Immanuelizing means coming to grips with the fact that *the medium is the message.* It means living up to our billing as the Body of Christ. Jesus said the world will know us because of our compelling lives of love (John 13:35). It means as individuals, and even more so as communities, taking on the character of Christ by exemplifying the fruits of the Spirit in all our dealings with others (Galatians 5:22, 23). In other words, our presence is love, joy, peace, patience, kindness, goodness, faithfulness, gentleness, and self-control.

Being present to others

Jesus did not hide from humanity — he moved right into our neighborhood. He profoundly identifies with us by becoming one of us. The gospel of John states, "And the Word became flesh and made his dwelling among us" (John 1:14). The word "dwelling" literally means tabernacling, or tenting. John alludes to the tent in which God's "shekinah" (visible presence and glory) dwelt with the Israelites from the wanderings in the desert to the construction of the temple. As God accompanied the Israelites through their journey to the Promised Land, so does Jesus accompany us through our journey of life. He stands in solidarity with us by his living, suffering, and dying alongside us.

Immanuelizing means being parish in a whole new way — moving from church as a Sunday event, or a series of programs, to church as presence. Instead of inviting people to events, we invite them into our lives. It means accompanying others on their journey by learning to rejoice with those who rejoice and weep with those who weep (Romans 12:15). It means building real relationships within the faith community and with those outside the parish.

Furthermore, Jesus' ministry was rooted within the fabric of the very culture in which he lived (weddings, funerals, feasts, work, etc.). Immanuelizing means entering the cultural life of the community around us and being the presence of God by deeply listening, truly understanding, and sincerely loving. In other words, we must reflect the same kind of genuine identification that God made with us in Jesus.

Living in humility

The incarnation represents the most profound act of humility in human history. The fullness of God's glory and power was hidden within Jesus and made subject to the very people and world he created. Instead of powerfully asserting his rights as God and coercing us into submission, he humbly emptied himself on our behalf. The Apostle Paul states it clearly:

> Do nothing out of selfishness or out of vainglory; rather, humbly regard others as more important than yourselves, each looking out not for his own interests, but (also) everyone for those of others. Have among yourselves the same attitude that is also yours in Christ Jesus, who, though he was in the form of God, did not regard equality with God something to be grasped. Rather, he emptied himself, taking the form of a slave, coming in human likeness; and found human in appearance, he humbled himself, becoming obedient to death, even death on a cross. (Philippians 2:3–8)

The immanuelizer wins hearts by selflessness, rather than spiritual or ecclesial stardom. Evangelistic credibility is the result of respecting others, rather than demanding respect because of positions or titles. Like Jesus, the immanuelizer's authority and power comes via humility and powerlessness.

Jesus not only embodied the most profound expression of humility, he taught us the way of humility. "The greatest among you must be your servant. Whoever exalts himself will be humbled; but whoever humbles himself will be exalted" (Matthew 23:11–12). When people exalt themselves by reminding us of their authority or accomplishments — whether verbal or through arrogant attitudes, our tendency is to not add an iota to an already exalted self. People who humble themselves by hiding their authority and refusing to mention their accomplishments instigate an opposite reaction. Because a humble person would never state what is obvious to everyone else, those surrounding him or her feel compelled to do so. Humility results in exaltation. Immanuelization works similarly. People respond to the gospel because of the credibility of selflessness, not the assertion of authority.

Modern Evangelization	Postmodern Immanuelization
Individual belief as evangelistic entry point	Community belonging as evangelistic entry point
Emphasis upon rational argument as the primary apologetic	Emphasis upon the life of the church as the primary apologetic
Emphasis upon individual questing (Good news for me)	Emphasis upon service evangelization (Good news for others)
Appeal of "having it all together"	Appeal of being together in our brokenness
The mission and agenda of evangelization	The mission of accompanying people

The Shift from "Evangelization" to "Immanuelization"

Moving from evangelization to immanuelization entails several essential shifts.

One is a shift from a focus on individual belief to community belonging as the evangelistic entry point. The current evangelistic approach primarily leads with an emphasis on the individual and personal belief. The individual made a choice of personally accepting Jesus through the sacrament of Confirmation, during a retreat experience, or through other activities, and then moved into full membership in the community. The map to a modern expression of faith often followed the sequential route of believing, belonging, and behaving. Driven by personally believing a certain set of religious truths, one then joined a community that shared the same individual beliefs, and then adopted the behaviors of the community.

Granted, community is in the very DNA of Catholicism. Our sacraments of initiation presume a supportive, surrounding community. We often criticized evangelical Protestant approaches that primarily emphasized a vertical "me and Jesus" evangelization. We rightly reminded them that they were "saved" into a community of faith. As a Church that is essentially ecclesial, we had the theology but often lacked the experiential reality. Over time we adopted an understanding of community as a disembodied theological truth that mostly fell short of authentic experience. Furthermore, many of our evangelistic endeavors tended to borrow from the successes of evangelical Protestants.[103] Practically speaking, many of our parishes became assemblies of individuals rather than authentic experiences of community.

Our evangelistic approach needs to shift from believing, belonging, and behaving, to belonging, behaving, and believing. If belonging is the evangelistic entry point, then evangelization must be rooted and expressed through the life of the community (as opposed to some individuals evangelizing for the community).

In the past, we've followed the believing, belonging, and behaving sequence. One embraces the faith, grows in the faith and community, and then gives away the faith. Mission or service was on the tail end and a mature response to one's belief. In reality, a faith journey is too rich and complex to be artificially packaged into a neat, predictable order. Young people today tend to hyperlink their way through life. Evangelization is not confined to particular evangelistic activities, but occurs in every corner of parish life as one is welcomed and participates in the overall life of the faith community. Because young people seek belonging and possess an embodied spirituality and a propensity towards active participatory activities, concrete and communal acts of service may be the most effective evangelistic activity.

Another shift is from rational argument as the primary apologetic to the life of the Church as the primary apologetic. As a young evangelizer, I dutifully studied numerous books on apologetics. I was impeccably prepared to argue as to why the Scriptures were trustworthy, the resurrection a sure fact, Jesus unique among world religious figures, and I could even demonstrate the historicity of the Catholic Church. I appealed to people's brains, providing reasoned arguments for the faith. I was eager to share my faith, packing an arsenal of pagan piercing apologetics. I was prepared.

That is, until the next generation of young people started showing up.

When it comes to discerning truth, today's young people speak a new language. The Church, as "the treasury of truths" leaves many of them shrugging their shoulders. Truth has to be real or work in real life to be true because they place more confidence in what they experience than what is merely said. In other words, truths are not judged by words and what makes rational sense, but by how well those words match up with real-life experiences. In order to effectively evangelize young people today, the life of our parishes must become our most convincing apologetic. The credibility of our message is directly tied to the quality of our love. Jesus was definitive about our identity and reputation in the world. He said, "I give you a new commandment: love one another. As I have loved you, so you also should love one another. *This is how all will know that you are my disciples, if you have love for one another*" (John 13:34–35, emphasis mine).

The early church understood that it was impossible to love and serve God without loving and serving God's creation. In the second century, the Christian apologist Aristides tried to win over the emperor Caesar Hadrian with the conduct of the Christian community. He spoke of how the Christians lived honestly and upheld the highest moral standards by comforting their oppressors and even making them their friends, doing good to their enemies, reaching out to widows, advocating for the safety of orphans, carefully burying the poor who have passed from this world, treating strangers like family, ministering to the prisoner; and fasting several days in order to get enough money to feed the hungry. If that wasn't amazing enough, he added that the Christians never announced their good deeds in public, but actually tried to conceal them, trusting their reward would come from their Messiah. He concluded by saying, "And verily, this is a new people, and there is something divine in the midst of them."[104]

Who can deny that there was something divine about these Christians? They so embodied the life and teachings of Jesus that he was truly present through them — the Body of Christ on earth. They were immanuelizing.

Being Church vs. Knowing Church

One of the Church's major disconnects with young people today is that we think religious knowledge is somehow going to win them back to the church. "If they only knew what we believe," we reason. The reality is that they do know what we believe. They've witnessed enough of it to not want it for themselves. Their indictment is chilling.

We need to deeply understand that the gateway to young people's hearts and minds is their experience of us as a community and force in the world. We are our best or worst apologetic for the faith. We need to rediscover what it means to be a community of disciples, who humbly love and serve one another and the surrounding world. We need to rediscover, on some meaningful level, how to relate to one another as a Christian community. So much of the new testament, especially the epistles, is simply about being church: Pray for one another (James 5:16); care for one another (1 Corinthians 12:24b–25); bear one another's burdens (Galatians 6:2); encourage & build up one another (1 Thessalonians 5:11); submit to one another (Ephesians 5:21); admonish one another (Colossians 3:16); spur one another toward love and good deeds (Hebrews 10:24); love one another (John 13:34). Few people would want to dodge a church with the above characteristics as its modus operandi. And, those from the outside might even break down the doors to gain entry.

Another shift is from emphasis on individual questing to service evangelization. Evangelical campaigns in the seventies and eighties featured slogans such as "Born Again" or "I Found It."[105] The messages of retreat movements and evangelistic conferences primarily appealed to the individualism of the age. Even the U.S. Army understood this, recruiting with the motto, "Be All You Can Be." Evangelization was primarily about "you" as an individual, and about your getting your eternity and inner self in good order.

The spirituality among young people today moves away from the individual questing that characterized many of the evangelistic approaches geared toward Baby Boomers and Gen Xers. The inner spiritual focuses hold less meaning, especially if outside the context of an authentic experience of community and concrete expressions of one's faith. Today young people prefer to express their faith in concrete and embodied ways. Inclusivity propels the heightened concern for justice among young people today. Justice and service provide teens with opportunities to address the needs of those pushed to the margins of society or those who have no voice. Teens gravitate towards doing service because it is done in the company of others, or in community. As a result, service is becoming the new face of evangelization.

Teens profoundly encounter Jesus in two ways as they serve. First, through the eyes of those they serve. With intentional theological reflection before and after serving, many teens recognize Jesus in the engagement — and are powerfully transformed as result. If evangelization is about facilitating an encounter with Jesus, there is no better place to find him than in the poor.

Second, young people fall in love with Jesus through his mission. They find the Great Lover as they love alongside of him. While joining him in his mission, they discover he's the real deal, the one person who has truly placed everyone else before himself, and they can't help but fall deeply in love with him.

From Eternal Kingdom to Present Kingdom

Earlier forms of evangelization catered to an individualistic spirituality. The evangelistic content was centered on the individual finding God's plan for their life and securing their own eternal salvation. The Enlightenment placed the human mind at the center of truth and removed religion from the public square of life. In turn, religion leaned towards a rational, cognitive understanding of faith and a focus on the heavenly Kingdom. Believers worked towards their eternal destiny, understanding their faith through universal propositions, and expressing their faith through personal morality. The "spiritually together" person was so caught up in the heavenly realm that they were unaffected by and independent of their surrounding historical circumstances.

Today's teenagers do not want to be evangelized to a set of ideas or rational truths, but to a practical reality. A faith that's mostly about you and your eternity isn't communal enough or concrete enough to warrant much interest. It's not that young people are uninterested in heaven or don't care about eternity. Rather, a life with little investment in loving and serving those around you seems pretty unworthy of heaven. The Kingdom of God is as much a present reality as an everlasting one. An evangelistic message that calls young people to sacrifice on behalf of others is an authentic message worthy of investing one's life.

Yet another shift is from having it all together to being all together in our brokenness. Earlier teens accepted a humanity characterized by independence, autonomy, and self-reliance. These highbrow notions trickled down into everyday cultural expectations. Fonzie, from the '70s television series *Happy Days*, was the poster child for the "together individual." The Fonz was cool, confident, and independent. He had it all together and had little need for others. Any fears or insecurities he may have harbored were safely masked beneath the image of his black leather jacket and Harley. The church had spiritual Fonzies. Holiness was defined by possessing a personal spiritual togetherness that separated you from others. Being holy meant having it all together, or at least projecting it. The holy person was busy with heavenly matters and less concerned with the contingencies of everyday, earthly business.

When gathering as a community, we connected on what we should be, not on what we were. One had to possess evangelistic credibility in order to bring people into this life-changing experience. That meant projecting an image of "having it all together" in order to attract those who didn't. Evangelization was about pretending you were complete in order to attract others to a "community" that pretended the same.

Instead of being transformed into the "together individual," the emerging spirituality seeks to be "together with others." Instead of connecting on being ideal believers, today's young people connect on their common brokenness. They lean away from overconfidence and certainty, and towards humility and mystery. Any display of religious swagger or moral superiority garners negative reactions. Practices that secrete even the slightest trace of religious arrogance — even with a benevolent exterior — are dismissed as toxic. Furthermore, any evangelistic approaches joined with narrow mindedness or intolerance are quickly shown the door. Equality and allowing everyone a place at the table is one of the highest postmodern values. Our brokenness keeps us all on a level playing field.

Finally there exists a shift from a mission agenda to one accompanying people. I had a friend during my college years who was so focused on the achieving the "great commission" that he was oblivious to his own "great omission" — the care of the very people at the center of his ministry. He loved evangelization more than the people he was evangelizing, and they knew it. People often felt they were a means to end, secondary to something greater, an achievement of *his* work. They felt quantified, objectified, and in the end emptied by the experience.

His approach was not uncommon. People were reduced to numbers, and programs replaced relationships. Furthermore, relationships were a means for "more important" agendas or were treated as a prerequisite for evangelization. Relationships, established as strategies of influence, left young people feeling demeaned as "projects." For example, the sacrament of Confirmation can take on a life of its own and become an end in itself. Once a program is set in motion, the program itself (instead of the people and purpose) can become the very focus.

Today's youth insist on inserting humanity back to the forefront of ministry. "Drive by" approaches have to give way to establishing genuine and trusting relationships with young people. Gun-shy from ubiquitous marketing, many young people smell insincerity or ulterior motives in a stranger's attempt to strike up a spiritual conversation. Instead of just inviting teens to our programs, we need to invite them into our lives. The immanuelizer is present and accompanies young people. The agenda is to love and walk with teens within the context of an embodied faith community.

It must be noted that "relationships without agendas" or being present to young people does not imply in any way that there is no place for proclamation when immanuelizing. What distinguishes immanuelization from some modern expressions of evangelization is that the relationship is not established for the purpose of proclamation. Proclamation occurs as a natural result of genuine and mutual relationships and within the everyday life of the faith community. A person remains loved whether they become a friend or enemy of the gospel.

Pope Paul VI was very clear when he wrote:

> The ministry of the word is a fundamental element of evangelization. The presence of Christianity amongst different human groups and its living witness must be explained and justified by the explicit proclamation of Jesus Christ the Lord. "There is no true evangelization if the name, teaching, the life, the promises, the Kingdom and mystery of Jesus of Nazareth, the Son of God, are not proclaimed."[106]

An Emerging Spirituality

In order to reach a new generation and the many adult tag-alongs, we need to acknowledge an emerging spirituality and respond with a new approach to evangelization, which I (and others) call immanuelization.

Immanuelization involves shifting our efforts from an individualistic and cognitive approach to faith to an authentically communal and experiential expression of faith. Immanuelization means moving from a program- and agenda-centered approach to a people- and presence-centered focus. Immanuelization means growing faith communities and youth ministries whose very nature is the most convincing apologetic. Immanuelization means rediscovering an embodied expression of the gospel, where our faith communities are an authentic Sacramental experience. Immanuelization means focusing upon building a powerful experience of affiliative faith as an essential foundation for successfully navigating searching faith and eventually landing upon owned faith. Immanuelization means attracting young people to Jesus because they experience his genuine presence in our community.

FOR CONSIDERATION

- When you hear the word "evangelization," what comes to your mind? What emotions, images, or experiences?
- If evangelization is the essential mission of the Church and the Church exists in order to evangelize, how well do you feel your parish is living out its mission?
- In light of the Catholic Church's decline in membership and church attendance, do you believe the Church is facing a serious crisis? Is your parish?
- When you hear the Church referred to as the "Body of Christ," what does it mean to you? In what ways do you experience (or not experience) this in your parish?
- Have you personally experienced "immanuelization"?
- Do you agree or disagree that service is the new face of evangelization? Please explain your reasoning.
- How can your parish best transition from evangelization to immanuelization? Do you think you should do so?

Notes

79. Jesus' final instructions to the Apostles, referred to as the great commission is the mandate to spread the gospel to all peoples (Mt. 28:19-20; Mk. 16:15; Acts 1:8).

80. Pope Paul VI gathered the 1974 synod of bishops around the theme of evangelization of the modern world. Based on that synod, he offered to the Church the landmark encyclical *Evangelii Nuntiandi* (On Evangelization in the Modern World) in 1975. *Evangelii Nuntiandi* helped shape a Catholic expression of evangelization by stating, "Evangelizing means bringing the Good News into all strata of humanity, and through its influence transforming humanity from within and making it new"(18).

81. Some material from this section is adapted from *Reflections on the Component of Evangelization*, Frank Mercadante © Center for Ministry Development, 2005.

82. *Go and Make Disciples: A National Plan and Strategy for Catholic Evangelization in the United States*. Washington DC: United States Conference of Catholic Bishops, 1993.

83 The U.S. Religious Landscape Survey: Religious Affiliation Diverse and Dynamic, 2008. Full report: http://religions.pewforum.org/pdf/report-religious-landscape-study-full.pdf.

84. Groups that have experienced the next largest net losses from changes in affiliation are Baptists (3.7%) and Methodists (2.1%). http://religions .pewforum.org/pdf/report-religious-landscape-study-full.pdf.

85. Ibid., page 24.

86. Ibid., page 29.

87. In recent years Catholics have actually become more comfortable with the word evangelization and increasingly more open to sharing their faith with others. Vatican II re-introduced the words evangelization, evangelize, and gospel into the Catholic vocabulary. Movements like the Charismatic renewal, Marriage Encounter, Cursillio, and parish evangelistic efforts like Christ Renews His Parish, Renew, and Disciple in Mission have flourished in many parishes nationwide.

88. Within the previous ten years, the largest number of adults choosing to become Catholic occurred in 2001 with 178,533 adults joining the Catholic Church. The number of adults joining the Catholic Church in 2009 was 124,404, the lowest number in ten years and a decrease of 30 percent from the 2001 total.

89. William V. D'Antonio et al. in *American Catholics Today* (Rowman and Littlefield, 2007, p. 55).

90. Mark M. Gray and Paul M. Pearl in *Sacraments Today, Belief and Practice among U.S. Catholics* (Center for the Applied Research in the Apostolate, 2008, p. 20). http://cara.georgetown.edu/sacramentsreport.pdf 91. Mark M. Gray and Paul M. Pearl in *Sacraments Today, Belief and Practice among U.S. Catholics* (Center for the Applied Research in the Apostolate, 2008, p. 20),

92. *Millennials A Portrait of Generation Next Confident. Connected. Open to Change.* 2010. Page 91. www.pewresearch.org/millennials.

93. David T. Olsen, *The American Church in Crisis.* Grand Rapids: Zondervan, 2008, page 175.

94. *Un Christian. What a New Generation Really Thinks about Christianity … and Why It Matters.* David Kinnaman and Gabe Lyons. Baker Books, Grand Rapids: 2007. Pages 24-25.

95. Ibid., page 42.

96. Ibid., page 27.

97. A well-known example is the author Anne Rice who announced her leaving the Catholic Church on Facebook: "For those who care, and I understand if you don't: Today I quit being a Christian. I'm out. I remain committed to Christ as always but not to being 'Christian' or to being part of Christianity. It's simply impossible for me to 'belong' to this quarrelsome, hostile, disputatious, and deservedly infamous group. For ten years, I've tried. I've failed. I'm an outsider. My conscience will allow nothing else." Whether one agrees with her or not, her announcement should not be ignored or dismissed by the church.

    Another published example is from an article in the *Chicago Tribune,* entitled, "Excommunicate Me, Please." See: http://articles.chicagotribune.com/2010-08-04/news/ct-oped-0804-excommunicate-20100804_1_excommunication-bishops-hierarchy.

98. CARA reports that 68 percent of Catholics at least "somewhat" agree with the statement, "I can be a good Catholic without going to Mass every Sunday." Mark M. Gray and Paul M. Pearl in *Sacraments Today, Belief and Practice among U.S. Catholics* (Center for the Applied Research in the Apostolate, 2008, p. 4).

99. *A Peculiar People: The Church as Culture in a Post-Christian Society.* Rodney Clapp. Downers Grove, IL: InterVarsity Press, 1996. Page 19

100. *Transforming Mission. Paradigm Shifts in Theology of Mission.* David J. Bosch. Orbis Books, Mary Knoll, New York, 1991.

101. Ibid., page 2.

102. *Finding Faith. The Spiritual Quest of the Post Boomer Generation.* Richard Flory and Donald E. Miller. Rutgers University Press. New Brunswick, New Jersey, and London, 2008.

103. A number of Catholic evangelistic organizations adapted Campus Crusade for Christ's Four Spiritual Laws as their methodology. The Charismatic Renewal was highly influenced by the Pentecostal movement.

104. The Apology of Aristides the Philosopher. Cited from http://www.earlychristianwritings.com/text/aristides-kay.html.

105. Many Baby Boomers were evangelized through campaigns with slogans such as "Born Again" or "I Found It." Even the U.S. Army utilized a similar approach with a "Be All You Can Be" recruiting slogan. Such approaches appealed to the individualism of the times.

106. *General Directory of Catechesis.* United States Catholic Conference, 1997 (50). The section includes a quote from Pope Paul VI in *Evangelii Nuntiandi* (On Evangelization in the Modern World) in 1975 (22).

CHAPTER SIX

RETHINKING ADOLESCENT CATECHESIS

I remember my own catechetical experience while growing up. After a grueling day at school, the buses rumbled in to pick us up for CCD (which was fondly understood to stand for "Church Captivity & Detention"). Like a funeral procession, we rode the bus in grim silence, looking despondent, as if our mothers had died earlier that day. Once the bus reached the "prison grounds," we moped our way to the classroom. We were "affectionately" welcomed by our instructor, who methodically snapped a ruler to her hand as a subtle reminder for us deviants to behave — or else. We knew there was only one escape route — and it was called "Confirmation!" (Okay, maybe there's a hint of hyperbole here.)

Many Catholic teens celebrate their freedom from ecclesial conscription via the gates of Confirmation. It's rather ironic that Confirmation celebrates an initiation into a church for which many immediately drop out. The truth is, we are failing to engage teens through our present approaches and methodologies.

When it comes to adolescent catechesis, we are often like the dog food company president who gathered all his employees for a big corporate rally. As he stepped to the podium, he was greeted with a spirited applause. He began his speech by asking his employees, "What dog food company has the best marketing program in the entire nation?"

His workers shot back by stating the name of their company with the kind of enthusiasm, excitement, and morale that would turn even an Amway convention green with envy.

On a roll, the president inquired, "Who, of all the dog food companies in the world, has the best employee incentive package?" One could physically feel the energy level rising in the room, as the entire throng exploded forth with the name of their organization.

Again, the president threw out another question to his faithful employees, "Who manufactures the most nutritious dog chow in this entire world?"

At a near frenzy, his audience screamed out with great pride the name of their beloved company.

The president paused for a moment as his employees leaned toward the edge of their seats. Surrounded with great anticipation, he lowered his voice and tempo, and quietly asked, "Why, then, are we not selling the most dog food in the world?"

Silence.

A stunned work force slumped back into their chairs. Still, silence.

Finally, a man in the back of the room slowly stood to his feet and shouted in response, "Because dogs don't like it!"[107]

We have the greatest news in the world, financial support, catechetical resources, and even dedicated catechists, but teens taste what we offer, don't like it, and fail to return (usually after Confirmation).[108]

A renewal in adolescent catechesis hinges upon a number of important shifts in our understanding, approaches, and practices. First, as previously discussed, the likelihood of effective faith formation increases when the parents of teens actively live and share their faith with their children. Second, the general vitality and youth friendliness of a parish community has a profound impact on teens. The chance of forming teens in a life-changing manner is dramatically increased when a parish fosters a vigorous affiliative faith within the community.

Head, Heart, and Hands

Perhaps one of the most challenging issues surrounding adolescent faith formation centers on our understanding of faith. For some, faith is primarily an enterprise of the mind. Good catechesis means passing on a cognitive understanding of the faith. Knowing what one believes constitutes effective catechesis. For others, faith is essentially a matter of the heart. Effective catechesis sparks a passionate, heartfelt relationship with Jesus. Finally, some people understand faith as an extension of the hands. The best catechesis results with one actively living and outwardly expressing his faith through concrete actions.

Historically, all three dimensions of faith are well represented in our Catholic tradition and spiritualities. The Scriptures also give ample evidence of each facet.

The head/mind:

"Do not conform yourselves to this age but be transformed by the renewal of your mind, that you may discern what is the will of God, what is good and pleasing and perfect" (Romans 12:2).

The heart/affection:

"And it happened that, while he was with them at table, he took bread, said the blessing, broke it, and gave it to them. With that their eyes were opened and they recognized him, but he vanished from their sight. Then they said to each other, 'Were not our hearts burning [within us] while he spoke to us on the way and opened the scriptures to us?'" (Luke 24:30–32).

The hands/action:

"For we are his handiwork, created in Christ Jesus for the good works that God has prepared in advance, that we should live in them" (Ephesian 2:10).

Moreover, Jesus braids head, heart, and hands into a single call when summarizing the great commandment to a scribe:

> One of the scribes, when he came forward and heard them disputing and saw how well he had answered them, asked him, "Which is the first of all the commandments?" Jesus replied, "The first is this: 'Hear, O Israel! The Lord our God is Lord alone! You shall love the Lord your God with all your heart, with all your soul, with all your mind, and with all your strength.' The second is this: 'You shall love your neighbor as yourself.' There is no other commandment greater than these." (Mark 12:28–31)

However, throughout history church leadership or movements have accentuated one aspect over others. Fifty plus years ago, the Church punctuated a more cognitive faith. Programs such as the *Baltimore Catechism* were popular and actually made good sense for the times. The *Baltimore Catechism* was a beautiful expression of the faith, supplying what was often missing for many Catholics at the juncture in history. Most Catholics lived in Catholic ghettos near extended families and attended Mass weekly. There was no question about belonging. Furthermore, they were surrounded by a homogenous faith community and culture that supported a Catholic lifestyle. The only ingredient missing was a basic cognitive understanding of the Catholic faith. The *Baltimore Catechism*, with its neat and tidy organization of religious facts, provided that. Because people of that time were skeptical of feelings, the heart dimension of faith was less emphasized. Because the surrounding culture generally supported a Catholic lifestyle, the behavioral dimension of faith did not need to be overly stressed. Given the context, the memorization of Catholic doctrinal propositions made sense. A catechetical approach highlighting knowledge and a cognitive understanding of faith worked for the times. But times have changed.

A Dire Diagnosis

The National Study on Youth and Religion conducted a thorough examination of contemporary teens and issued a dire diagnosis. Most teens, particularly Catholic teens, demonstrated an incredible inability to articulate the basic teachings, beliefs, and practices of the faith.

Our knee-jerk, pendulum-swing, impulse reaction might be that time traveling back to a yesteryear form of catechesis, as exemplified by the *Baltimore Catechism*, to a time when Catholic teens could actually tell you what they believed, seems to be just what the doctor ordered! But the times have changed, radically changed. Alone, a head dimension of faith, or any single expression of faith, is simply too anemic for our present context. True, many of our Catholic teens don't know the faith, but many aren't living it[109] or expressing it through a deep interior life,[110] either. Fifty-plus years ago we primarily had a deficit in a single dimension — the cognitive knowledge of the faith. Today, all three facets suffer from underdevelopment.

Communication Eras and Learning

Recent catechesis has generally been one of two styles: Print and Electronic, which is further divided into Broadcast/Digital. We tend to gravitate towards the communication style most reflective of the era in which we grew up. Change has occurred so quickly in recent years that we may have catechists or religious education approaches from each of the styles.

Print Era Learning

A print era approach veers towards a classroom-like structure that is organized around content and objectives. Typically, information transfers vertically from the teacher and the learning texts to the students. The print era teacher tends to communicate content abstractly, factually, and in linear fashion. Favorite teaching mediums include individual study, lecture, and reading of texts.

Broadcast Era Learning

Broadcast communications emerged with the advent of film and later television. Like television programming, information is conveyed visually, linearly, produced by experts, and entertaining. A broadcast era approach organizes the classrooms around the needs of individual students. Teachers are more experience-centered, utilizing text learning, but supplementing with additional learning mediums like movies, videos, and activities such as group presentations and discussions. Teachers may rely on edu-tainment approaches, such as delivering presentations with emotional stories, humor, and dramatic effect. The broadcast era teacher maintains the responsibility for learning along with some ancillary support from students via participation.

Digital Era Learning

Digital era learning emphasizes a collaborative learning environment. In more of a horizontal fashion, the community shares the responsibility for teaching and meeting the needs of individual learners. Content is highly participative, interactive, and experiential. Learning flows more randomly, through dialogue, focuses less on information and more on reflection, integration, and incarnation of that information. Dramatic delivery gives way to authentic sharing; abstract principles give way to narrative; expert authority gives way to everyone having something to share.

Teens have been formed through their Internet experiences, hyperlinking their way through content, responding to feeds, leaving comments after articles, uploading their self-produced videos, and playing Internet games. Information is a ubiquitous commodity that's easily accessed — the greater need is to know how to sort and work with the content.

Transitioning towards a digital era approach to learning does not mean amputating content or not having a scope and sequence to catechesis. These remain critical components for effective adolescent catechesis and all of education for that matter. Our beliefs, traditions, and teachings need to be passed on in a systematic manner.

Young people need to practice a whole faith, where all three dimensions work together in a concerted and mutually supportive fashion. The faith of the head finds its best expression when one's heart abides in the presence of God, and one's mission reflects the love and ways of Jesus. The passion of one's heart is best channeled when embanked by sound Catholic teaching, and expressed in concrete acts of love. Actions of witness, mercy, justice, and service most fully embody our faith when empowered by a heart of passion, and directed by a cogent theology. The best catechesis forms teens in a living spirituality, a solid theology, and an outwardly expressed mission. A whole faith, and therefore, a whole catechesis address the head, heart, and hands of teens.

Understanding that effective catechesis involves the head, heart, and hands is a good place to start, but there are also some important nuances for the present generation. As John Dewy said, "If we teach today's students as we taught yesterday's, we rob them of tomorrow."

Authentic catechesis involves the transmission of authentic Catholic teaching. It does not mean elevating opinions and personal experiences to the level of revelation. It does, however, mean making every attempt to enflesh the meaning of the gospel by making real-life, experiential connections. It means shifting the focal point of our content from inert, disembodied facts towards life-implication and integration — "a period of formation, an apprenticeship in the whole Christian Life."[111]

Moreover, a digital era of catechesis does not mean a well-trained and educated catechist has nothing more to share than a fourteen-year-old. Following Jesus' example, our authority expresses itself through humility and is recognized through our sharing, modeling, and embodiment of the teachings of the Church. Additionally, it means opening the door for teens to be the body of Christ, using their gifts in a meaningful way to share and build up one another.

Catechetical Challenge: So What? Who Cares?

In an article entitled, *Wake Up and Smell the New Epistemology*, sociology professor Tim Clydesdale offers his fellow professors some helpful insights on teaching young people today.

In many ways, he describes the present educational playing field as a convergence of postmodern epistemology and digital technology. He says students do not "drink deeply of notions like 'knowledge for knowledge sake.'" He challenges instructors to neither blame nor scorn this generation, but to genuinely respect them as persons and thinkers. He says, "They have become exactly what one would expect of those born during the information age and reared in America's profoundly pragmatic culture." Young people have grown up with the world at their fingertips — literally. They both easily access and are endlessly assaulted by ubiquitous streams of information. Their instantaneous access to knowledge levels the intellectual playing field, undermining the authority of the expert. Moreover, they know they can find authorities for every position and information claim, making them dubious of what others attribute as true or important. Their accessibility of information does not intimate they have become skilled masters of knowledge and interpretation. It only means they have become savvy at "sorting, doubting, or ignoring the same." In the end, Clydesdale summons instructors "to see the two questions that the new epistemology emblazons across the front of every classroom — 'So what?' and 'Who cares?' — and then to adjust their teaching accordingly."[112]

Clydesdale's insights have broad implications for adolescent catechesis. One is that we can safely assume that most teens will not stand in awe of us as catechists, nor defer to the Church as an authoritative institution with an authoritative message for their lives. Demanding authority will only backfire with a generation that has little covert respect for position or title. In many ways, we are in a similar position to the early church. Surrounded more by contempt than authority, they established their credibility via their self-sacrificing love for people.

Today, young people recognize authority in authenticity, transparency, and connectedness, and generously return respect when genuinely respected. We need to approach our students as colleagues and our classrooms as communities. Moreover, we would do well by transitioning from being the "sage on the stage," to becoming the "guide on the side."[113]

Another thing we must do is to prepare for every session by asking ourselves "So what?" and "Who cares?" The very act of asking these difficult and challenging questions prepares us beyond any catechetical resource. They drill through to our own being, penetrating the depths of our hearts, striking and releasing the wellspring of our own passion for what we believe, and the stories that incarnate those beliefs. Rather than pontificating on impersonal truths, we witness to their personal reality in our lives — a perspective young people need today.

Today's young people understand truth as more personal and practical than objective and propositional. When experience serves as the primary sifter for truth, real life becomes the lab for determining it. In other words, young people want to know if this stuff works. The onus is on us to demonstrate that it, indeed, works. Taking this position doesn't mean that we embrace the notion that "truth is simply what works." Nor does it imply that we do not recognize God's innate authority. It simply means providing teens with a good look under the hood of God's ways, helping them recognize that love motors all of God's motives. Behind every negative commandment of God stand two positive and practical purposes: protection and provision. Every "No" is undergirded by a big, fat, emphatic "YES!" Yes, God wants what's best for us. God's commandments, like riverbanks, provide protective boundaries. When a river flows within those boundaries, communities flourish. When waters exceed their boundaries, like a flood, they wreak pain, havoc, and destruction.

Experience and Reflection

After working full-time for a couple of years, my Millennial Generation son, Michael, was offered a new job over a thousand miles away. As he was preparing to move, he proudly conveyed to me that he could fit everything he owned into his car. I responded, "You've worked full-time for two years and you can fit everything you own in your car?" He looked at me incredulously and said, "Dad, I'm not into things. I'm into experiences!"

Millennials are collectors of experiences. Knowledge was the coinage of the modern world, but experience is the currency of a postmodern culture (of which Millennials are native citizens). Again, this makes for a very interactive and participatory approach to life and learning. Teens have always complained about stationary, passive learning, but the protests have hit a crescendo with the Millennials. Today's teens are not content with gathering knowledge about God from an expert. They hunger for an encounter with God and to experience God personally. They do not want to learn about the tenets of prayer as much as experience the presence of God through prayer. They are less interested in lectures on Catholic social teaching than being immersed in a real-life mission — where they personally experience the face of injustice.

Modern learning tends to begin in the mind, seeking to gain knowledge by studying the facts. Once the facts are understood, one might consider the practical application of those facts. Millennials often work in reverse. They begin with the application and afterwards come to understand the facts by reflecting on the experience in light of the Scriptures and Catholic teaching. In other words, the past generations were more prone to reflection and then action, while this generation is more inclined to action and then reflection.

Because Millennial teens hunger for an experiential faith, it's important that at times our catechesis leads with experience, but never ends there. Experience without knowledge results in a theological shallowness. Good catechesis offers spiritual experiences that help make the faith real, but grounds those experiences in the language and tradition of our Catholic faith.

The best catechesis combines socialization and religious experience. Socialization occurs when teens learn within the environment of their families and parishes the Catholic tradition — the symbols, stories, practices, and prayers, etc. Religious experience involves those powerful moments where teens feel they personally encounter the presence of a living God.

Carol Lytch, in the book *Choosing Church*, summarizes the interaction of the two:

> When a teen is attracted to participate in his or her church over time, religious commitment (or loyalty) is fostered in a circular process by which socialization and religious experience mutually build on one another. Because youth have the symbols, stories, and practices to use to interpret their experiences as religious, they are enabled to name experiences of God as such. Congregations that both socialize youth into religious traditions and create conditions where teens feel they experience

God tend to have teens who exhibit religious commitment.[114]

Peer Affiliation

TRUE: Teenage Millennials enjoy closeness to their parents that the previous generation lacked.

TRUE: They are more influenced by their parents and often ascribe a parent with hero status.

FALSE: They are not highly influenced by their peers.

Peers matter, and the parishes that understand this capitalize upon it by building strong, cohesive bonds among teens in the community. Youth ministry approaches that segregate teens into their own exclusive communities have come under fire in recent years. The critique has nothing to do with the practice of gathering teens together with peers. Young people still want and need to assemble with people their own age. The criticism has more to do with the exclusivity of the practice, at the expense of a robust family and intergenerational ministry. Growing a highly connected youth subculture within and the larger experience of parish affiliation represents a win-win scenario. There remains incredible power in peer pressure. Most often, we associate it with negative teen conduct, such as alcohol or drug abuse, gang involvement, or violence. Indeed, numerous studies have established the link between peer pressure and teen criminality. Driven by the need for acceptance and the hunger for belonging, young people will barter destructive behaviors for the respect and esteem of their peers.

The abuse of Iraqi detainees in the Abu Ghraib prison became one of the most publicized international news stories during the Iraq war. Twenty-two-year-old army reservist Pfc. Lynndie England pleaded guilty to two counts of conspiracy,

four counts of mistreating detainees, and one count of der-
eliction of duty. The widely circulated photos of her grinning
and giving the "thumbs up" sign next to naked and humili-
ated Iraqi prisoners symbolized everything that went wrong
at Abu Ghraib. During her trial, England conceded she knew
the abuses were wrong, but went along with them because of
peer pressure. She told the judge, "I had a choice, but I chose
to do what my friends wanted me to. They were being very
persistent and bugging me, and I was like, okay, whatever." [115]
In the end, England was sentenced to three years in prison.
One can only conclude that fitting in and garnering the respect of one's peers is a powerful behavior-changing agent.

The same behavior-changing power exerts influence in
a positive direction. Peer pressure can redefine popular but
risky behaviors as unattractive choices. It can declare un-
popular practices such as chastity as attractive and desir-
able. Peer pressure can persuade teens into believing and
accomplishing something they would never consider possible outside the group. Margaret Mead once said, "Never
doubt that a small group of thoughtful, committed, citizens
can change the world. Indeed, it is the only thing that ever
has."[116]

In the book, *The Rise of Christianity*, sociologist Rodney
Stark contends that the explosive growth of the early church
was not the result of believers seeking or embracing Christian ideology as much as it was a result of social attachments.
He writes, "Attachments lie at the heart of conversion, and
conversion tends to proceed along social networks formed by
interpersonal attachments...."[117]

Twenty-first-century adolescent catechesis must first intentionally build a deep experience of peer-to-peer connection and genuine Christian community. Alone, information

renders little effect. Ask any smoker. Ask a person who drinks or gambles too much. Each day, people engage in risky, even life-threatening behaviors, with full knowledge of their potential consequences. Now, add a teenage brain to the equation, where their prefrontal cortex, that area of the circuitry that links behaviors to consequences, is late to mature. What teens need most is a community whose shared beliefs, norms, and ways of living insulate them from considering crazy adolescent behaviors — behaviors they may not link with future negative consequences. Therefore, it is imperative to develop communities where youth experience belonging, feel valued, are respected, and are encouraged to explore their dreams. This intentional "school of community" is far more beneficial than a rote classroom environment. Within the relational context, information is valued, embraced with others, and provides an experience of solidarity.

The experience of community is formative in and of itself. Learning how to build up, encourage, support, speak the truth in love, contribute one's gifts, appreciate the gifts of others, and love annoying people forms us into Christ-likeness like nothing else.

More Than Good Intentions

My primary experience with youth ministers, catechists, and priests is that they are passionate about impacting young people and fervently desire to pass on the Catholic faith and are sacrificially trying to do so. If intentions could build vibrant and life-changing youth ministries, there would be thousands of them throughout our country. But as we know from experience, it takes more than good intentions. Our parishes need to understand and apply the basics of forming affiliative faith, providing learning opportunities that combine the head, heart, and hands, utilize teaching approaches that effectively engage teens and offer positive peer influence within a welcoming adult community if we are to effectively meet the needs and challenges of the next generation.

FOR CONSIDERATION

- From which communication era (oral, print, broadcast) do you primarily operate? From which communication era does your parish's adolescent catechetical program primarily operate?

- In what ways might your catechetical approaches shift towards a digital expression without losing the most valuable approaches of the past?

- What might be the results if catechetical programs, talks, or homilies began with these questions "So what? Who cares?"

- If older generations are more prone to reflection and then action, while young people are more inclined to action and then reflection, what might be the implications for adolescent catechesis? Which does your catechetical program presently lean towards?

- In what ways does your parish community socialize young people into the faith? How can this be done more effectively?

- In what ways does your faith community provide powerful religious experiences for young people? How can this be done more effectively?

- In what ways does your parish's catechetical efforts capitalize on peer affiliation? In what ways can you further develop a sense of community among teens?

Notes

107. Adapted from *Up Close & Personal. Wayne Rice Youth Specialties, Inc.* Zondervan Publishing House, Grand Rapids, MI, 1989. Page 14.

108. Adapted from *Growing Teen Disciples, Strategies for Really Effective Youth Ministry*. Frank Mercadante. St. Mary's Press, 2002. Pages 158–159.

109. Fifty-eight percent of Catholic teens reported that their religious faith was only somewhat, not very, or not important at all in shaping their daily life. National Study of Youth and Religion: Analysis of the Population of Catholic Teenagers and Their Parents. Charlotte McCorquodale, Victoria Shepp, Leigh Sterten. A Research Report Produced for The National Federation for Catholic Youth Ministry, December 2004. Page 34.

110. Ibid., pages 26, 27, 28. Only one-third of Catholic teens reported feeling extremely or very close to God; half of all Catholic teens never read the Bible; only 34 percent pray at least once a day.

111. *General Directory for Catechesis*, #63

112. *Wake Up and Smell the New Epistemology*, by Tim Clydesdale. http://chronicle.com/article/Wake-UpSmell-the-New-E/4568/January 23, 2009.

113. Saying was coined by Alison King, Professor of Education at California State University, San Marcos. *From Sage on the Stage to Guide on the Side in College Teaching*, Volume 41 #1, 1993, pages 30-35.

114. *Choosing Church. What Makes a Difference for Teens.* Carol E. Lytch. Westminister John Knox Press, 2004. Quoted from page 199.

115. http://articles.latimes.com/2005/may/03/nation/na-lyndie3.

116. Quote from Margaret Mead. Although often used, the exact origin of this quote is unknown and believed to have been in a newspaper report of a statement she made spontaneously and informally. It is, however, a reflection of a concept she expressed often.

117. *The Rise of Christianity A Sociologist Reconsiders History*. Rodney Stark. Princeton University Press, 1996. Quoted from page 18.

CHAPTER SEVEN

PREPARING THE SOIL
OF LEADERSHIP

This chapter concerns leadership, because leadership is everything. As much as we may want to ignore it or try to work around it, great leadership remains critical to building a great parish and a great ministry with youth. Unfortunately some leaders are like Enhanced Radiation Warheads.

More popularly known as the neutron bomb, this is one of the most feared and loathsome weapons ever conceived and developed for modern warfare. A small tactical thermonuclear weapon, the neutron bomb produces minimal destruction when detonated. By removing the uranium casing of a hydrogen bomb, the neutrons that are released travel expansive distances, penetrating armor and thus delivering a lethal dose of radiation. In the end, buildings and equipment remain standing without a sign of human life. Its inventor, Sam Cohen, describes it this way: "The most detested weapon on earth, far more so than the hydrogen bomb.... The neutron bomb is one of the most discriminative weapons ever devised."[118]

Over the years, I have seen some pastoral leadership changes that have had a similar spiritual effect. Lively ministries that took years to build, parish leaders that took considerable exertion to form, authentic communities that took intentional effort to develop were destroyed by a new leader in a relatively short period of time. Every sign of spiritual life was gone, but program structures, church buildings, and equipment remain standing. In order to avoid that, we need to look at some key issues surround leadership.

The Cultivation Process

For the past twenty years, I have led a youth ministry organization named Cultivation Ministries. Some may surmise the name comes from our Midwest location, where rolling cornfields dominate the landscape. Actually, the name comes from the agricultural metaphor we use as a descriptor for the process of building a disciple-making parish and youth ministry. Relatively few of us make a living as farmers, but most of us have some experience with growing some kind of plant or garden. We know that in order for a plant to bloom or bear fruit we must prepare the soil, sow the seeds, and tend to its growth. The same holds true for building a high-yield, fruitful parish and youth ministry.

In order to grow a disciple-making parish and/or youth ministry we must:

Prepare: develop leadership

Sow: evangelize

Grow: spiritually form

Reap: equip, empower, and mobilize ministers and leaders

Prepare

Bottom line, the goal of every farmer is a harvest of abundant fruit. The same can be said of discipleship. In John 15:8, Jesus said, "By this my Father glorified, that you bear much fruit and become my disciples." Fruit is central to discipleship. In the end, we want to grow a community of disciples who bear abundant fruit.

However, the harvest always begins with the soil. A barren, and underprepared soil results in either no harvest or a sparse harvest. Conversely, a carefully tilled, fertilized, and aerated soil significantly increases the odds of ending with a rich and healthy harvest. The soil represents the leadership behind the disciple-making efforts. A parish increases the odds of producing fruit by carefully cultivating leadership and ensuring that it has certain compositional qualities.

Sow

Once the soil is prepared, the farmer sows seeds. Sowing represents the process of evangelization/immanuelization. A parish continually sows the seeds of faith in such ways as incarnating the love of Jesus in the community, proclaiming the gospel message during gatherings, facilitating encounters with the living Christ through powerful spiritual experiences, equipping parents to share their faith with their children in their homes, and sharing the good news through meaningful relationships. The goal of sowing is spiritual germination — in other words, coming to the realization that in order to live one must die. Conversion occurs when one dies to self and lives for Christ. God is the cause for any growth (1 Corinthians 3:6–7). Still, the farmer has an important partnering role with God — doing everything he or she can to create the right conditions for germination.

Grow

Once a plant germinates, the farmer's energies turn to new tasks, with the aim of promoting healthy growth and development. Those duties may include watering, fertilizing, weeding, and chasing away annoying crows. Grow represents faith

The Cultivation Cycle[119]

Movement	Focus	Goal
Prepare	Leadership	Develop a nutrient-rich soil of leadership that will lead to a future harvest
Sow	Evangelization Immanuelization	Foster ongoing conversion
Grow	Faith and spiritual formation	Nurture faith and spiritual maturity
Reap	Equipping and exercising ministry and leadership	Reproduction of new leaders who live the mission of the Church

and spiritual formation. Activities involved in this movement include catechetical formation, spiritual development, family catechesis, digital catechesis, parish liturgies and other gatherings. In the end, grow is all about nurturing maturing faith in others.

Reap

To reap is the ultimate goal of the farmer. All previous efforts lead to this end — the bearing of fruit. Fruit is a by-product of maturity and characterized by other-centeredness and activities of mission. Reaping involves helping young people discover, develop, and exercise their gifts in ministry and leadership. The movement includes equipping, empowering, and mobilizing ministers and leaders in ministries such as evangelization, justice and service, catechesis, liturgical ministries, and the like. The cultivation process ends where it began, becoming a cycle of reproduction. The process begins in the ground (Prepare), where seeds lose their lives (Sow), to only flourish and grow (Grow), and reproduce the process in others (Reap). From a spiritual perspective, the process moves young people from spiritual consumer to world transformer. Young people move from "Jesus, what can you do for me?" to "Jesus, what can you do through me?"

Preparing the Soil

The whole process of cultivating a community of teen disciples is contingent upon a well-prepared soil, or in other words, a great youth ministry leadership team.

Ministry Team Model

A youth ministry leadership team can be organized in a number of different ways. I work from a model where the leadership team is primarily composed of a coordinator/animator of youth ministry and directors of specific ministries. This group gathers monthly in order to report on the progress of the ministries and address the larger picture issues that impact the mission and strategic mapping of the youth ministry. In turn, each director has his or her own team who meets and carries out its specific ministries. Over the course of the year, the entire youth ministry team, comprised of the coordinator/animator, ministry directors (leadership team), and all the youth workers in each of the ministry teams, gather occasionally for training, community building, spiritual formation, and so on.

So what makes a great youth ministry team? What nutrients need to be present on every level of leadership in order to ensure a future harvest? Effectively preparing the soil involves discipling the disciple-makers; sharing a Spirit-led vision and plan; developing a community of ministers; effective group processes; and a reliance on the power of God through intercessory prayer.

Discipling the Disciple-Makers

Parishes can spend a small fortune on well-designed catechetical resources, without investing significant time forming and training adult catechists. That is like purchasing a Formula One racecar and having a ninety-nine-year-old with cataracts at the wheel. Sure, one needs a good car to win, but that car will likely crash and burn without a competent driver. When I think of the most significant moments in my own faith formation, I think of people — how they listened, loved, and responded to me. It may have been in a formal context, with organized curriculum, but it was always people who made the content come alive in their stories, insights, and manner in which they embodied gospel. Spiritually forming and feeding our leaders is tantamount to life-impacting youth ministry. It takes a disciple to make a disciple.

When training youth ministry leaders on a number of occasions, I have asked, "How many of you feel that your parish offers ample and effective opportunities for nurturing your own spiritual growth?" At best, I have witnessed 10 percent of the participants raise their hands. On several occasions, no one raised their hands.

For too long, we have adopted the "strip mining" approach to volunteer ministry. That's when we strip unassuming volunteers of all their time, energy, and spiritual resources, and then leave them emotionally exhausted, spiritually hollow, and totally burned out.

The spiritual calories burned through the exercise of their ministries should be replenished through the spiritual growth opportunities within the general life of the parish or through specific gatherings for ministry volunteers. The best-case scenario involves ministers who are spiritually nurtured by participating in the life of the parish. But, if the leaders do not seem to be receiving sufficient spiritual nourishment, it's critical that we supplement their feeding during gatherings with catechists or ministry leaders.

Bottom line, our leaders need to be spiritually fed and cared for pastorally. Discipleship is the foundation for Christian leadership. What our leaders are is a pretty good indicator of what our young people will become.

Spirit-led Vision and Plan

As Catholic youth ministry has evolved over the past decades, so have the titles used to describe the role of the parish youth minister. Initially, the parish youth minister was simply called the "youth group leader." The title reflected the role — an individual who ran the youth group. With the publishing of *A Vision of Youth Ministry* in 1976, second-generation Catholic youth ministry introduced the term "coordinator of youth ministry." This title communicated the shift towards a comprehensive and team approach to youth ministry. The leader's role was to coordinate the various ministry programs led by parish volunteers on the team.

More recently, some leaders have suggested shifting the title to "youth ministry animator," to reflect a new understanding of the role. The research of the *Effective Youth Ministry Practices in Catholic Parishes* project revealed that it takes much more than the mere coordination of programs to be an effective leader in parish youth ministry. The best leaders lead spiritually. They contribute a sense of inspiration and vision, along with the coordination of tasks.

I have served as a youth ministry volunteer over the years. When a compelling and shared vision was missing from a ministry, so were adult leaders (once their children were done) and teens (once confirmed). A lack of vision always ends with volunteers feeling frustrated. It is like joining a competitive basketball team whose coach sees the games as mere recreation. Before long, you feel like you're wasting your time, energy, and talent because the team is going nowhere.

Clear and Compelling Destination

Ministries need destinations. Leaders and ministers need to gather around a purpose worthy of their energies and efforts. Teams need a compelling vision — a spiritually discerned, visual picture of what God desires for the teens of their community. It's not enough to buy a program that worked someplace else, invest in some curriculum written by experts, or to go through the motions of ministry as they have always been done in the parish.

God has a plan for your community. Prayerfully discerning it provides the inspiration for achieving it. A team discovers and touches the heart of God when communally discerning its mission. One of the most exciting moments of that plan involves the process of prayerfully identifying it. Team members realize that they're not simply writing a mission statement, but their work is the work of a living God who deeply cares and has a plan for the young people of their community. That realization changes everything. A team begins to believe they are on a divine mission led and fueled by an omnipotent God. Their job is to cooperate with the Holy Spirit. Now, that's a lot more exciting than running a program!

Destination with Directions

While in high school I asked an attractive girl out on a first date. I decided we would spend a whole day at Cedar Point, a large Ohio amusement park about an hour drive from my home in Cleveland. I picked up my date early in order to arrive at the park by opening. After driving a distance, I remember seeing a sign on the turnpike that read, "Cedar Point Right Lane." So I moved into the right lane. I remained in the lane until I reached the border of Indiana (two hours later). After paying my toll, I asked the tollbooth employee, "Is Cedar Point up the road?" He had a good laugh. Pointing, he said, "It's a couple of hours back in the direction you came!" I felt pretty stupid at that point. To make matters worse, my date hopped into the backseat and fell sound asleep. We finally arrived at Cedar Point at 4:30 in the afternoon. I chose a great date destination. However, by the time we got there we were in no mood to enjoy it.

A youth ministry team will go nowhere without a destination. However, even with one, they may never arrive at that destination without good directions. Or, take so long to get there that they end up too exhausted and frustrated to even appreciate it. A mission spells out what we aim to achieve, but a strategic map shows us how to navigate our context. Mapping our way to the destination by planning, and developing structures and goals, is critical to effective leadership.

A shared vision offers a leadership team hope, purpose, direction, and inspiration. Taking the time to spiritually discern a destination and carefully map the routes to get there is a critical element in a well-prepared soil. (Appendix B provides some direction on how to develop a strategic map.)

Community of Ministers

Young people hunger for deeper connection and experience of community in their parishes. This remains a distinguishing, yet often unaddressed characteristic of an emerging spirituality among teens. The effective ministry team intentionally builds community among its members. Investing the time and energy to grow strong and meaningful bonds among team members pays rich dividends in several important ways. However, the hunger for belonging is not exclusive to teens. Adults seek the same experience for themselves. Providing a rich expression of community within the context of ministry ensures that we address adult spiritual needs as well. Moreover, ignoring the appeal of relationships and organizing teams primarily around tasks will result in a higher leader attrition rate. Giving up a set of tasks associated with a ministry role is much easier than leaving people whose lives you have entered and who have entered yours; people with whom you have prayed, shared, worked, and loved. Building a community among those with whom you minister remains one of the most significant deterrents for the volunteer revolving door syndrome that plagues many youth and religious education ministries. Moreover, when a team shares a Spirit-guided mission and loves working together, you have a combination that naturally retains leaders. A lively community with an inspiring mission will not only help preserve existing team members, it will persuasively draw future members as well.

Furthermore, in order to foster community among teens, adult leaders need their own authentic experience of community. Based upon their previous involvement in parish life or religious education, many adults may operate from a classroom or content-focused paradigm. Offering an experience of genuine community within the context of leadership can be formative in and of itself. In the end, it serves as a model for community, helping leaders foster the same experience with teens.

In order to grow an authentic ministerial community, leaders must reserve time during leadership meetings, and/or arrange social gatherings or retreats solely for this purpose. Often, I will begin a meeting with the question, "What is God doing in your life?" or, "How is everyone doing?" If a member shares an issue in their life requiring prayer, I routinely pause the meeting and ask the group to intercede for that member. Sometimes the prayer is followed up with more listening, encouragement, support, or even practical advice from others in the group. Occasionally, an issue may require practical support outside of meetings, such as providing meals while a family member is hospitalized. In the end, my hope is to build a community of ministers who truly love one another, knowing how to "Rejoice with those who rejoice, weep with those who weep" (Roman 12:15).

Now, with that said, it remains critical that teams appropriately manage their community building. Spending entire meetings building relationships among team members, praying for one another, and singing endless songs, yet never getting to the needs of teens, amounts to the greatest failure. Keep meetings focused on your ministry purpose and keep your meetings in balance.

Effective Group Practices and Processes

An effective youth ministry team must share a personal commitment to discipleship, to one another as a community, and to a compelling youth ministry vision. However, if the way a team gets things done is routinely characterized by dysfunction, there remains little chance they will ever see a harvest. For instance, if a team can't make decisions, follow through on decisions made, problem-solve, or manage conflict, it is essentially doomed.

Every leadership team has its own way of getting things done. These processes or routines include how meetings are run, decisions are made, information is communicated, problems are solved, accountability maintained, and conflict is managed. When a team's communication processes are carried on in an effective manner, it actually enhances the overall positive experience of team members. When processes are done poorly, they become a source of frustration or even despair for team members. Let's just say you're in trouble if your team meetings have no agenda, endlessly whirl, jump from topic to topic without ever coming to closure, and always end with the church janitor telling you, "It's one in the morning and I have to lock up now!"

Dependence on Prayer

Sometimes we fail to recognize the value of what we already possess. It's easy to miss what's below the surface. Take, for example, the man who sold a painting of a dismal country scene at a Pennsylvania flea market to a collector for four dollars. The price seemed fair. However, the seller was unaware that behind the frame stood an "unspeakably fresh copy" of a first printing of the Declaration of Independence. The document was beautifully preserved as a result of being sealed and folded up. Not long afterwards, the new owner received $2,420,000 at an auction for his four-dollar investment.[120] The new owner was lucky. But, consider the guy who sold him the painting!

Essential Processes

Community must go beyond personal connection to effective ways of working together in order to accomplish the mission. Here are some essential routines or processes.

Meeting agenda

Assemble a manageable and realistic agenda beforehand. In order to stay on task, assign specific time allotments for each agenda item. Don't include concerns that can be effectively addressed through other means (emails, newsletters, etc.). Send the agenda to members in advance and allow them an opportunity to include additional items. Make sure you include time for community building or any spiritual or ministry formation. Hand out copies to members during the meeting. Follow the agenda during meetings.

Effective meeting facilitation

A well-crafted agenda needs a skilled facilitator. Otherwise, it becomes an exercise in futility. Like a traffic cop, a meeting facilitator needs to keep the group moving, avoiding bottlenecks, and eventually ensuring that everyone gets home on time. Effective facilitation includes staying on task and completing agenda items within the allotted time; making sure everyone participates and shares; making sure one person does not dominate the conversation; affirming the contributions of team members; managing conflict and differing opinions; providing clear instructions; summarizing, clarifying, and bringing closure; and all the while creating a warm and affirming community among members!

Sometimes, the coordinator may not be the best facilitator. Don't sacrifice the team over it; work with the natural

Continued on next page

gifts and skills within the group and find another member to facilitate the meetings.

Decision-making processes

A youth ministry team will always make decisions: some minor — such as the color of a retreat team t-shirt; others major — such as which teens will be chosen to serve on the retreat team. Matching the decision with the right decision-making process becomes an important skill. Teams may use any of the following decision-making methods:

- Voting: Used for low-importance decisions, such as the color of a shirt. Voting ensures a team doesn't waste time on decisions of little consequence.
- Expert: Used for a decision that requires some technical expertise, such as the choice of a new sound system or projection unit. The team essentially delegates the decision to an individual or group who possess the expertise needed.
- Consensus: Used for high-importance decisions that requires everyone's support, such as offering a new program or ending an old one. Consensus may not reflect everyone's first choice. However, no one has any serious reservations and everyone feels they can support the decision.
- Communal Discernment: Used for high-importance decisions that require careful discernment of God's will, such as the choice of a new leader, or mission statement. Communal discernment is a labor of prayer. The group seeks the Holy Spirit's decision on a matter. In the end, the team must be in unanimous agreement with the choice.

In the end, a team wants to make the best decision, in the shortest amount of time, with everyone's full support, and still liking one another afterwards.

Accountability

An important task of a leader involves establishing, developing, and protecting a team's morale. A team with high morale exercises greater confidence, accomplishes greater things, and feels great about their participation on the team. Morale begins forming within the first few meetings. Members' gauge the team's potential and possibilities based on the group's early performance. When a team realizes that they can count on one another to do things well, follow through on what they have agreed to do, and accomplish great things together, the group will enjoy high morale. In turn, high morale tends to perpetuate the same positive team behaviors that produced the high morale in the first place. The team enters a winning trajectory.

The leader's role is to help the team believe and have confidence in one another. This happens by fostering accountability. From the very first meeting with a new team, I am straight about the yin and the yang of obligations. A high-performing team, and the accompanying high morale, begins by forming a highly appealing vision that demands high team expectations. Great expectations require high team standards. High team standards are maintained through mutual accountability. A great youth ministry is deeply committed to honest self-evaluation. If they have developed a depth of community, and share in a compelling vision, they have the foundation to weather the kind of criticism that in turn leads to greatness.

Continued on next page

Communication

A team's manner of communication involves how members interpersonally communicate with one another and how information is exchanged regarding ministry events, decisions, meetings, and the like.

I can know a lot about a team without ever hearing any words. Body language speaks volumes. In actual fact, most of our communication is nonverbal. Some basic gestures of respect for one another can positively enhance a team's experience. A great team embeds the following practices into their culture: making soft and warm eye contact with a member who is speaking; turning one's head and leaning one's body towards the speaker; using attending skills when listening, such as nodding to indicate that you are with a speaker; using short brief indicators that you are following a speaker, such as "Mm-hmm"; not interrupting a team member when she is speaking; asking questions when to better understand what a team member means; and summarizing what others have shared in order to clarify understanding.

A second form of team communication involves sending essential information out to team members in an effective, clear, and timely manner. Communications items vary, but may include: team meeting reminders, meeting minutes, "to do" reminders, and other forms of basic information. Communicating well involves finding the best mediums (for example, email, website, Facebook, Google Groups, mail, etc.), using the best formats (such Word attachments, PDFs, etc.), writing information clearly, and getting the information out in a timely manner.

In the end, when a team communicates well, they save considerable time and energy by eliminating the need for the "meeting after the meeting." The "meeting after the meeting" is a secondary gathering or discussion where team members share how they really feel and is usually indicative of some form of team dysfunction.

Conflict management

Conflict is inevitable. When conflict arrives uninvited, the first step involves welcoming it. Avoiding conflict only ensures that it grows deeper and expresses itself in other covert ways.

If a team invests in building community and in the previously mentioned routines and processes, they proactively eliminate a considerable percentage of potential conflict. Moreover, offering team training that provides members with both a protocol and practical skills for dealing with conflict will prove to be very helpful.

He gave up his chance to be a multimillionaire for a measly four bucks. What a tragedy! If only he knew what was behind that dismal piece of art! How different his life would be!

Too often, this story describes parish leadership. We can fail to recognize the value and power of what God gave us in intercessory prayer. Sure, prayer can seem dreary and mundane at times, but hidden beneath the familiar is world-history-changing power. Leadership teams that deeply understand this, change the history of their young people and parishes.

Every church has hidden within its membership parishioners who have the gift of intercession. Within our ranks, often concealed by older age, introversion, or even a lack of ministry involvement, are the "history changers." Because we often fail to utilize the resource of intercession in our ministries, we fail to deploy these valuable parish ministers.

Anthony De Mello so wisely said, "It is only at the end of this world that we should realize how the destinies of persons and nations have been shaped, not so much by the external actions of powerful men, and by events that seemed inevitable, but by the quiet, silent, irresistible prayer of persons the world will never know."[121]

Most of us believe in prayer. We know we should regularly pray for our teens and ministries, but often get caught up with the practical aspects of youth ministry. Instead of feeling guilty, we need only to recognize that we were not given the gift of intercession. Not having a gift for intercession doesn't mean we don't pray on behalf of others, it only means it is not our primary ministry. Instead, look for members of the parish who have the gift and are willing to use it on behalf of the parish's teens. Be proactive in prayer by organizing a team of intercessors who regularly intercede for the teens, youth ministry leaders, and youth events. Treat intercessory prayer like other ministries by recruiting a competent director and team. Develop goals such as having every teen in the parish prayed for daily by at least one person. The team that makes the ministry of intercession a priority by organizing a team that actively prays for the teens, leaders, mission, and efforts of the youth ministry, will experience a powerful move of God.[122]

Self-Replicating Leadership

A youth ministry is well on its way to an abundant harvest when a youth ministry team ensures that its members are well-formed as disciples; propelled and guided by a shared purpose; enjoy deep connections as a community of faith;

benefit by and have full confidence in the team's systems, processes, and operations; and sense the power of God profoundly working through a dependence upon prayer.

Moreover, a team characterized by the above qualities has a certain effect on ministry recruiting. It reduces the need for begging, pleading, and tearfully imploring from the pulpit. It ensures you never have to resort to inducing guilt, and finally threatening to shut down the whole program if someone — anyone (with a pulse) — doesn't volunteer! No one wants to leave a great team, and everyone wants to join one. The best recruitment happens innately — by simply doing things well.

Third-Generation Youth Ministry Leadership

Preparing the soil by cultivating a great youth ministry team remains essential. Building a youth ministry that sows, grows, and reaps is critical to growing teen disciples. Establishing a youth ministry structure that reflects the cultivation cycle by planting the seeds of faith through evangelizing/immanuelizing, fostering faith and spiritual growth through various formational ministries, and bearing fruit by equipping and providing teens with opportunities in leadership and ministry is all a part of growing a disciple-making youth ministry. However, transitioning into third-generation youth ministry requires moving away from a microlevel, independent ministries approach, to a macrolevel, interdependent ministries paradigm. Engaging the next generation demands that we turn our focus towards growing an engaging parish from the youngest to the oldest members of our faith communities. It means cultivating an entire parish of disciples by continually sowing, growing, and reaping.

In order to engage a new generation of teens, we must understand the changes that make this generation "new." In many ways, a cultural tsunami has rendered our old youth ministry maps obsolete. In order to find our way and remap a ministry with teens, we must become familiar with the new territory. Understanding the characteristics that distinguish the Millennial Generation, and learning the implications of a digital culture are keys to reaching today's teens. In light of these changes, we need to think creatively and discover new ways to lead (Prepare), evangelize (Sow), catechize (Grow), and form new leaders (Reap).

Moreover, in order to engage a new generation of teens, young people will need to become a pastoral priority. The National Study on Youth in Religion, Exemplary Youth Ministry study, and the Effective Youth Ministries Practices in Catholic Parishes research found that the best ministries with

A New Collaboration

Collaboration means something very different in today's environment. Leadership models need to shift focus from individual ministries towards the common areas among ministries — the networks, relationships, interactions, and the interdependencies of ministries. Collaboration needs to begin with the overriding purpose of parish discipleship.

Furthermore, leaders need to adapt their approaches to reflect the present interactive and interdependent environment. Modernity gave us Newtonian physics, where laws were observed. The new physics is more participatory in nature. Physicist John Wheeler says, "The universe does not exist 'out there,' independent of us. We are inescapably involved in bringing about that which appears to be happening. We are not only observers. We are participators. In some strange sense, this is a participatory universe."[123]

young people occur in congregations that make youth ministry a high priority. From staff members to the parishioners, the congregation understands that youth ministry remains everyone's responsibility. Moreover, the parish seeks to incorporate young people into every aspect of the community.

Finally, we must transition from running independent, separate ministries, to an approach that recognizes the interdependencies of all of parish life, with discipleship of all parishioners as a common goal. Third-generation Catholic youth ministry fundamentally understands that the vitality of our faith communities, and our ability to foster an affiliative style of faith are foundational to engaging the next generation.

FOR CONSIDERATION

- "Leadership is everything." What does this mean to your youth ministry?
- In what ways are your parish and youth ministry preparing, sowing, growing, and reaping? Can you identify programs, activities, events, and relationships that address each of these movements? In which movements are you strong? In which do you need to improve?
- How well does the parish or youth ministry produce leaders who personally embrace discipleship? In what ways is your parish youth ministry spiritually feeding those who serve? In what ways might you improve your support and spiritual formation of your leaders?
- On a 1 to 10 scale (1 being low and 10 being high), how would you rate the clarity of your parish's youth ministry destination or vision? How would you rate your parish's directions or strategic map to get you there?

- In what ways can you improve on the experience of community among the adult leadership team?
- Of the following communication and team processes (meeting agenda, meeting facilitating, decision-making, accountability, communication, and conflict management), which is functioning best? Which needs the most work? What can be done to improve your team's processes?
- In what ways are your young people and ministry to youth being supported by active intercessory prayer? In what practical ways might it be improved?
- How would you rate your youth ministry team's ability to self-replicate? What is most attractive about your team? What needs the most work?
- How would you rate your parish's overall collaboration in making disciples of all generations?

Notes

118. http://www.youtube.com/watch?v=z_QFXGxw6Tk. Interview with Sam Cohen.

119. For a detailed development of each of the Cultivation process movements, see the book, *Growing Teen Disciples: Strategies for Really Effective Youth Ministry*. Frank Mercadante. St. Mary's Press, 2002.

120. http://www.nytimes.com/1991/06/14/arts/declaration-of-independence-sells-for-2.4-million.html.

121. *Sadhana, A Way to God: Christian Exercises in Eastern Form*, by Anthony De Mello. Image Books Doubleday, 1978. Quoted from page 124.

122. For more practical details on how to build an intercessory prayer ministry , see chapter five in the book, *Growing Teen Disciples: Strategies for Really Effective Youth Ministry*. Frank Mercadante. St. Mary's Press, 2002.

123. Physicist John Wheeler, quoted in *The Voice of Genius: Conversations with Nobel Scientists and Other Luminaries*. Denis Brian. Page 127.

CHAPTER EIGHT

INSPIRATION FROM NEHEMIAH AND MATCHMAKING

Maybe your parish can't boast of hundreds of enthusiastic teens stampeding their way into your youth ministry events. Perhaps it seems like the parents in your faith community have little more interest than steering their children through sacramental motions. Maybe the spiritual vitality of your parish is best described as on "artificial life support."

Don't despair. The history of the Church is filled with turnaround stories of such situations. Moreover, the Scriptures paint vivid stories of hope and transformation. *We can make a difference.*

Be Like Nehemiah

Nehemiah, a Jewish layman, worked as a cupbearer for the Persian King Artaxerxes after the exile. Deeply moved by the fact that Jerusalem laid in physical and spiritual ruins, Nehemiah was granted permission by the king to rebuild the walls of Jerusalem. Nehemiah's story suggests a helpful six-part template for changing a culture.

1. Prayer

The book of Nehemiah is set in motion when Nehemiah gets wind of the situation in Jerusalem and of his surviving countrymen living there. The headlines are dreadful. Disgraced and disillusioned, the residents of Jerusalem remain vulnerable and defenseless, their walls gutted and exposed. Nehemiah's kneejerk reaction was to turn to God in prayer. "When I heard this report, I began to weep and continued mourning for several days; I fasted and prayed before the God of heaven" (Nehemiah 1:4).

Nehemiah's prayer, recorded in the remainder of chapter one, concludes with, "O LORD, may your ear be attentive to my prayer and that of all your willing servants who revere your name. Grant success to your servant this day, and let him find favor with this man" (Nehemiah 1:11).

Shortly afterwards, Nehemiah was serving wine to King Artaxerxes and his prayers were answered. The king sensed sadness in Nehemiah and probed. Nehemiah revealed his despair over the situation in Jerusalem. The king responded by asking, "What is it, then, that you wish?" Nehemiah paused and prayed. Then he asked the King if he might travel to Judah and rebuild the city. Nehemiah's initial prayer was answered as the king gave both permission and provision for the task (Nehemiah 2:8). Later, while immersed in the work, Nehemiah continued to depend on the power of prayer while navigating the many obstacles that threatened to halt the progress of rebuilding (Nehemiah 4:3).

Like Nehemiah, when seeking to rebuild a parish culture into a youth-friendly, disciple-making experience, our beginning, our middle, and our end is prayer. I learned this, somewhat by accident, as a young college graduate hired to my first parish youth ministry job.

I was hired full-time in a new parish that had no previous history of youth ministry. With no adults to train, teens to work with, or programs to maintain, I had a lot of time on my hands! Figuring I better look busy (and spiritual), I began every single day by praying for every single teen by name. I certainly wasn't going through the motions; I cared about reaching teens with the Gospel, and I believed in the power of prayer. However, to be totally honest, I am not sure I would have invested as much time in prayer if I had to begin working with both feet running. Because of my unique situation, I stumbled "by accident" upon a truth that never left me — prayer works! I couldn't have possibly, in any way, used my time better.

During the course of that first year, I witnessed what could only have come from God. Our first youth gathering began that summer with a meager twelve teens. By the end of the school year, that same gathering was bustling with more than 120 young people. By themselves, large numbers say very little. The real story was the culture of discipleship being formed. It began with young person after young person trying to express to me in his or her own words either a faint spiritual ache, or longing for more, or of a hole that this world was too tiny to fully satisfy. They were longing for Jesus and joined discipleship groups to learn how to know, love, and serve him. The Holy Spirit was answering those prayers and transforming our culture.

Any real change in parish culture must begin and be sustained in active prayer. Our inclination to leap frog to the "practical" often blinds us to our most powerful resource. Begin here. Depend on prayer. Build and organize a coalition of intercessors who actively pray for teens, parents, parish vitality, clear vision, and leadership. In the end, prayer remains not only the first, but also the most practical of steps.

2. Passion

Nehemiah was not only rooted in prayer, he was fueled by passion. The word passion originates from the Latin term *pati*, meaning "to suffer." While reading the Book of Nehemiah, you can't help but feel his longing for the people and city of Jerusalem. Nehemiah's tone throughout the book conveys passion. He suffers with yearning and the pain of restrained desire. He provides us with a textbook definition of passion. In other words, we have to want something so much that the unfulfilled desire is a source of suffering or hurt. Furthermore, passion motivates — supplying the emotional drive necessary to rally the troops toward change.

3. Perspective

Nehemiah had perspective, or vision. The difference between a dreamer and a visionary is perspective. A visionary confronts the present reality. A dreamer ignores it. Nehemiah began by walking the perimeter of Jerusalem and assessing the present reality (Nehemiah 2:13–15). He saw for himself the demolished walls and the fire-damaged gates. However, that's not all he saw, nor was it his primary focus. A "Dreamer" may not acknowledge reality, but a "Drainer" embraces it in high definition. In the end, a Drainer drowns others by submerging them under a whirlpool of the overwhelming obstacles. Nehemiah, neither a dreamer nor a drainer, was aware of the present reality and turned his focus toward a prayer-inspired, alternative future.

Nehemiah's culture-changing perspective was baked with three key ingredients. First, it was formed through prayer (Nehemiah 2:12). Psalm 127:1 reminds us, "Unless the LORD build the house, they labor in vain who build." Second, a culture-changing perspective is fully aware, but not utterly overwhelmed by the present reality (Nehemiah 2:17). Third, a culture-changing perspective is passionately propelled by a visual picture of what could be (Nehemiah 2:17, 18).

4. Partnership

Nehemiah was prayerful, passionate, and had visionary perspective, but he was equally a realist. Even with God's assurance and the king's full support, he knew he didn't have a complete hand for the task. He drew from the deck by inspiring others to join the effort. (Notice this was Jesus' first move in his ministry as well.) He began with a few people three days after he arrived (Nehemiah 2:12). As he passionately relayed the vision God had put into his heart, the numbers supporting the work swelled (Nehemiah 3:1–32).

Whether we are a boss or a laborer, like Nehemiah, we need to gather a network of passionate partners willing to intercede, interact, and implement. Gathering together a community fueled by their passion for young people enables youth ministry leaders to establish the organic, grassroots efforts necessary in today's environment. People want to know that their voices are heard and are true partners in the vision, not just worker bees for the alpha leader.

At some point, however, the pastor must get involved. EYM research demonstrates the crucial role of the pastor. Maybe, like Nehemiah, our first intercessory focus is to find favor and support from our pastor. Although it is not necessary for the pastor to be involved in every detail, his example, support, and advocacy cannot be underestimated.

5. Plans

After assessing the damaged walls and gates, Nehemiah shared his vision:

"You see the evil plight in which we stand: how Jerusalem lies in ruins and its gates have been gutted by fire. Let
us rebuild the wall of Jerusalem, so that we may no longer be an object of derision!" Then I explained to them
how the favoring hand of my God had rested upon me,
and what the king had said to me. (Nehemiah 2:17–18)

The people responded to Nehemiah's vision saying, "Let
us be up and building!" (Nehemiah 2:18). Shortly afterwards,
the vision was fulfilled as each section of the wall and gates
were assigned to different individuals, families, and tribes.

Again, a vision remains inert and only a dream when
ignoring reality. Equally, a vision is only unrealized sentiments when lacking practical expression. A vision only grows
wings and takes flight when fleshed out into concrete plans
and practices. Engineering a practical plan for parish cultural
transformation is an essential step. (*The Faith Assets Assessment* in Appendix A can be a helpful tool for assessing unique
needs and developing a plan.)

6. Persistence

Finally, even with prayer, passion, perspective, partners, and
a set of plans, you will need patience and persistence. Prepare
yourself for a road littered with potholes, downed lines, and
barricades. Nehemiah had his — in the form of the mocker-
ies, threats, plots, intimidations, uncooperative countrymen,
unjust practices, and unrest stemming from those practices
(Nehemiah 3:33–35; 4; 5). The work of rebuilding almost
came to a halt as workmen cradled weapons with one hand
and construction tools with the other. Further difficulty
emerged between countrymen as the powerful took financial
advantage of the poor.

The journey towards culture change is slow, demanding, and exhausting. Overwhelming obstacles will threaten your vision. Be patient and present; the harvest comes in due season. While cultivating, personally embody the values and vision of the emerging culture. If you want the parish to be more hospitable, be an example of friendliness and hospitality. If you feel relationships need to be more real, model authenticity and sincerity. Effective leaders of change create a sense of safety for allies and adversaries alike, listen attentively, and discern which threads can be safely pulled and which should remain untouched because they may unravel the entire fabric of the parish. Remember, culture transformation is rooted in cooperating with the Holy Spirit, not in wrestling political control and seizing power.

We, like Nehemiah, are called to do our part in rebuilding a temple worthy of the Lord. He prayed, sought direction, joined with others, and did the work that was in front of him. We, too, can change our parishes and youth ministries by beginning with ourselves. If we are willing to seek God in prayer, be part of a larger community committed to discipleship, and let go of our own agendas so that we can be open to God's will, we can truly become part of the solution.

Transitioning to Third-Generation Catholic Youth Ministry

Beyond Nehemiah's inspiration and leadership template, how can a parish engage this new generation? How can a faith community transition to effective third-generation youth ministry? I believe it's by becoming matchmakers.

Several years ago, a former Cultivation Ministries' employee travelled from Washington State to visit my family. Casey brought his wife Lisa and their two small children. I was particularly thrilled to see little Lucy and Oliver for the first time. You see, they were the products of my matchmaking! Yes, I am a matchmaker.

Several years earlier, I was helping with production at a diocesan youth rally. Working with me was Casey. Alongside of us sat an attractive young woman (close to Casey's age) and her father. They were running the PowerPoint presentations for the diocese.

I immediately picked up on a few things. Lisa was pretty, faith-filled, and enjoyed being with her father. Seemed like a pretty good eligibility combination to me. As the day progressed, I thought I was sensing, on her part, some interest in Casey. That was my cue to spring into action!

On the sly, I whispered, "Casey, you need to get this girl's number!" The disinterested bachelor shook his head. (Sometimes these kinds of matters require a tad of persistence.) So, I reiterated my sentiments again, and again, and — okay — maybe again. Casey rolled his eyes.

I was resigned to defeat as we loaded the last of our equipment in a now empty room. It was then that Casey waved a small piece of paper in my face. With a twinkle in his eye he confessed, "I got her number."

Today, it's all matchmaking history. And now, batting 1000, I am ready to call the Church to the ministry of matchmaking. As a matter of fact, the key to engaging a new generation is transitioning from teachers to matchmakers. We match-make in three important ways.

1. Matchmaking Young People to Jesus

First, the matchmaker arranges opportunities for young people to meet Jesus. As youth ministers, we help facilitate encounters with Jesus — experiences where teens meet, get to know, and fall deeply in love with Jesus. Instead of saying prayers, we lead teens into a meaningful interaction with Jesus; instead of singing songs, we lead teens into a real experience of worship; instead of just sharing in small groups, we learn to listen for the Holy Spirit in the words of one another; instead of simply performing service, we discover the presence of Jesus through the eyes of those we serve. When we do this, we transition from religious activities to real and meaningful encounters with the presence of Jesus. At its very core, evangelization is about a personal encounter with the risen Lord.

Furthermore, effective matchmakers know both parties well. Matchmaking involves a high level of trust. Those being matched need to trust that the matchmaker knows the person with whom they are being matched. Therefore, Jesus can't be a stranger or a distant friend to the matchmaker. The matchmaking evangelizer lives as a disciple of Jesus, placing him before every other interest in their lives. The credibility needed requires an intimate, personal knowledge of Jesus. Sharing our own personal stories of Jesus helps others become more interested in meeting him. Speaking of our own experiences with Jesus, and his influence in our lives, paves the way for those being matched to meet him.

Secondly, the matchmaker must know the person being matched. They need the assurance that you know them well before they will ever trust you to match-make. The best evangelization flows from meaningful, caring relationships. When we enter into the lives of young people, truly listen to them, accompany them through their struggles, we begin to understand their spiritual hungers. Whether it's the hunger for love, belonging, purpose, completion, forgiveness, or to make a difference, Jesus is the match to their hunger. Genuinely investing in the lives of teens, discerning the pull of their souls, and drawing them to Jesus to whom their souls long is the real stuff of evangelization.

2. Matchmaking Young People to the Parish Community

Modernity, with its exaggerated emphasis on individualism, disconnected people from their innate communal rooting. Today, postmodern young people long for meaningful connection and the experience of authentic community. Belonging is the gateway to conversion. It is through the credibility of the community, forged through meaningful attachments, that young people will embrace the call to discipleship. Within community, young people draw on the example, spiritual strength, and faith understanding of significant others. The experience of being loved and being a part of a community where your gifts are mined, refined, and utilized lays the road to personal and owned faith.

Matchmaking young people to the community may mean adopting more of a relational spirituality. Whether pastoral leaders realize it or not, many parishes primarily communicate an institutional spirituality by emphasizing bricks and mortar, financial needs, and parish upkeep. Or in another model, we may largely function with a maintenance agenda, reinforcing nominal expressions of cultural Catholicism by inadvertently emphasizing sacramental hoop jumping. The best Catholicism has to offer is neither institutional nor cultural — it's relational. It's about falling in love with Jesus, sharing that love with one another, and extending that love to the world around us.

We must match-make young people and their families to the community by fostering connections with other families and members of the parish. These connections should be made in the larger community, within family ministry, and within age-segmented ministries. The key is intentionality. Virtually every gathering or meeting can include time to foster connections, from greeting those around you before Sunday Mass, to including mixers, life and faith sharing, shared prayer, etc. within common programming.

Moreover, young people need adult and peer mentors in their lives. They need faith-filled people to apprentice them into the faith by investing in their lives. We must organize our youth ministries in a manner that makes safe and appropriate relational practices our *modus operandi*. By growing a team of adult and teen peer ministers that value relationship building, are trained in relational ministry, and are held accountable for practicing it, we can build a kind of relational culture that has the best potential to grow lifelong disciples.

3. Matchmaking Young People to their Vocation

Finally, we match-make young people to their call, mission, and vocation. By becoming a relational parish and youth ministry, we can better get to know the young people in our community. As a result of collectively interacting with teens while being involved in small groups and various parish and youth ministries, we begin to see growing tendencies and budding passions in young people. Their personalities blossom, gifts emerge, and skills develop. As twenty-first-century pastoral ministers, we add another dimension to our role as leaders: helping teens discover their gifting, calling, mission, and vocation within the context of the faith community. We take on the role of a spiritual miner, trying to help teens discern their gifts and calling by sifting through what we have observed and learned through interacting with them. Sharing our observations, encouraging teens when we see them doing something special, pointing them in potential directions, recommending particular books or websites, and praying with them for vocational discernment are common practices of the vocational matchmaker. Helping teens discover and meaningfully use their gifts within the community and mission of a parish deeply roots them in their faith and within the community.

Teens can't help but feel loved by the community when members invest so much in their lives. They can't help but feel an important part of the community when their gifts contribute to the overall life of the parish.

When we match-make young people with Jesus, the community, and to their gifting and calling, we address the most significant spiritual longings of teens today. Young people hunger for transcendence — to know and to be known by an all-loving God. Young people long for authentic community — to be meaningfully connected to others and to give and receive love. Young people hunger for purpose — to live their lives meaningfully and to fulfill their God-given destiny. When a parish focuses on this kind of matchmaking, they will be successful in engaging a new generation.

I am going to be a *matchmaker*. How about you?

FAITH ASSETS

Faith Assets Assessment[124]

(Assessment should include a one to five scale on "priority of importance" and "practice effectiveness.")

The Faith Assets can provide a common language to involve all members of the congregation in discovering their role in the lives of young people. Use this assessment tool to reflect on the *priority* and *practice* of the Forty-Four Faith Assets in the life of your congregation and youth ministry. The Assessment Tool can be used with church staff, key leadership, and leadership councils to conduct an overall assessment of the congregation's impact on young people. It can be used by the youth ministry team, as well as by church staff and key leaders, to assess the effectiveness of the youth ministry effort. The tool is best used in group settings where there can be discussion and shared analysis. Begin by giving people time to complete the assessment individually. Then, use the following process to share reflections and analysis, and plan for improvement in each of the four asset groupings.

Assessment Process

Select your first Faith Asset grouping for analysis: (1) Congregational Faith and Qualities; (2) Youth Ministry Qualities; (3) Family/Household Faith; or (4) Leadership.

Develop a profile of current practices and activities for this Faith Assets grouping: *How does our congregation (as a whole community, as a youth ministry, and/or as leaders) promote these Faith Assets?*

Develop a composite score of the group's assessment of the *priority* of the Faith Assets in this grouping. (How important is this asset to our congregation?)

Discuss the reasons for people's ratings using the following questions: (a) *Is this an accurate picture of our congregation's priorities in this asset area?* (b) *Why do we believe it is accurate or inaccurate?* (c) *Should a particular asset be a higher priority than it currently is?*

Develop a composite score of the group's assessment of the *practice* of the Faith Assets in this grouping. (How well are we doing in this area as a congregation?)

Discuss the reasons for people's ratings using the following questions: (a) *Is this an accurate rating of our congregation's practices in this asset area?* (b) *Why do we believe it is accurate or inaccurate?* (c) *How does our rating compare with the quality and scope of our specific activities for these Faith Assets? Which assets do we need to develop more fully?*

Identify the Faith Assets in this grouping that your congregation needs to make a higher priority and/or develop more effective practices.

Plan for improvement to strengthen the Faith Assets that you have identified as important areas of growth: (1) Brainstorm potential strategies to develop the Faith Asset; (2) Select one or more strategies for action; and (3) Develop an action plan with implementation steps, budget, leadership, and dates for completion.

Part 1: Congregational Faith and Qualities

Congregational Faith

Asset 1: God's Living Presence: The congregation possesses a sense of God's living presence in community, while at worship, through study, and in service.

Asset 2: Centrality of Faith: The congregation recognizes and intentionally participates in God's sustaining and transforming life and work.

Asset 3: Emphasizes Prayer: The congregation practices the presence of God as individuals and community through prayer and worship.

Asset 4: Focus on Discipleship: The congregation is committed to knowing and following Jesus Christ.

Asset 5: Emphasizes Scripture: The congregation values the authority of Scripture in its life and mission.

Asset 6: Centrality of Mission: The congregation consistently witnesses, serves, and promotes moral responsibility, and seeks justice.

Congregational Qualities

Asset 7: Supports Youth Ministry: Youth and ministry with young people are high priorities.

Asset 8: Demonstrates Hospitality: Values and welcomes all people, especially youth.

Asset 9: Strives for Excellence: Sets high standards, evaluates, and engages in continuous improvement.

Asset 10: Encourages Thinking: Welcomes questions and reflection on faith and life.

Asset 11: Creates Community: Reflects high-quality personal and group relationships.

Asset 12: Encourages Support Groups: Engages members in study, conversation, and prayer about faith in daily life.

Asset 13: Promotes Worship: Expands and renews spirit-filled, uplifting worship through the congregation's life.

Asset 14: Fosters Ethical Responsibility: Encourages individual and social moral responsibility.

Asset 15: Promotes Service: Sponsors outreach, service projects, and cultural immersions both locally and globally.

Asset 16: Demonstrates Effective Practices: Engages in a wide variety of ministry practices and activities.

Asset 17: Participate in the Congregation: Youth are engaged in a wide spectrum of congregational relationships and practices.

Asset 18: Assume Ministry Leadership: Youth are invited, equipped, and affirmed for leadership in congregational activities.

Part 2: Youth Ministry Qualities

Asset 19: Establishes a Caring Environment: Youth ministry provides multiple nurturing relationships and activities resulting in a welcoming atmosphere of respect, growth, and belonging.

Asset 20: Develops Quality Relationships: Youth ministry develops authentic relationships among youth and adults establishing an environment of presence and life engagement.

Asset 21: Focuses on Jesus Christ: Youth ministry's mission, practices, and relationships are inspired by the life and ministry of Jesus Christ.

Asset 22: Considers Life Issues: Youth ministry values and addresses the full range of young people's lives.

Asset 23: Uses Many Approaches: Youth ministry intentionally and creatively employs multiple activities appropriate to the ministry's mission and context.

Asset 24: Is Well Organized and Planned: Youth ministry engages participants and leaders in long-range planning, implementation, evaluation, and innovation in an atmosphere of high expectations.

Part 3: Family and Household Faith

Asset 25: Possess Strong Parental Faith: Parents possess and practice a vital and informed faith.

Asset 26: Promotes Family Faith Practices: Parents engage youth and whole family in conversations, prayer, bible reading, and service that nurture faith and life.

Asset 27: Reflects Family Harmony: Family members' expressions of respect and love create an atmosphere promoting faith.

Asset 28: Equips Parents: The congregation offers instruction and guidance that nurture parental faith and equips parents for nurturing faith at home.

Asset 29: Fosters Parent-Youth Relationships: The congregation offers parent-youth activities that strengthen parent-youth relationships.

Part 4: Leadership

A. *The Pastor*

Asset 30: Spiritual Influence: The pastor knows and models the transforming presence of God in life and ministry.

Asset 31: Demonstrates Interpersonal Competence: The pastor builds a sense of community and relates well with adults and youth.

Asset 32: Supports Youth Ministry: The pastor understands, guides, and advocates for youth ministry

Asset 33: Supports Leaders: The pastor affirms and mentors youth and the adults leading youth ministry.

B. *The Youth Minister*

Asset 34: Provides Competent Leadership: The youth minister demonstrates superior theological, theoretical, and practical knowledge and skill in leadership.

Asset 35: Models Faith: The youth minister is a role model reflecting a living faith for youth and adults.

Asset 36: Mentors Faith Life: The youth minister assists adult leaders and youth in their faith life both one-on-one and in groups.

Asset 37: Develops Teams: The youth minister reflects clear vision and attracts gifted youth and adults into leadership.

Asset 38: Knows Youth: The youth minister knows youth and changes in youth culture and utilizes these understandings in ministry.

Asset 39: Establishes Effective Relationships: The youth minister enjoys effective relationships with youth, parents, volunteers, and staff.

C. Youth and Adult Leadership

Asset 40: Equip for Peer Ministry: Youth practice friendship, care giving, and outreach supported by training and caring adults.

Asset 41: Establish Adult-Youth Mentoring: Adults engage youth in the Christian faith and life supported by informed leadership.

Asset 42: Participate in Training: Youth and adults are equipped for ministry in an atmosphere of high expectations.

Asset 43: Possess Vibrant Faith: Youth and adult leaders possess and practice a vital and informed faith.

Asset 44: Demonstrate Competent Adult Leadership: Adults foster authentic relationships and effective practices in youth ministry with a clear vision strengthen by training and support.

Notes

124. The Faith Assets Assessment is taken from *The Spirit and Culture of Youth Ministry: Leading Congregations Toward Exemplary Youth Ministry.* Roland Martinson, Wes Black, and John Roberto. EYM Publishing 2010. Pages 68-74. Used with permission from John Roberto.

Cultivation Strategic Planning Model

Done in the context of Christian Community

Mission

Broad and over-riding purpose; Reason for existing; Final Destination. Rooted in the mission of the Church. Answers the question: **What** are we about?

Needs

The specific profile of your community: interests, attitudes, schedules, lifestyles, influences, etc. Answers the question: **Whom** are we seeking to reach?

Vision

Mission and needs interact with one another to form a visual picture of what effective ministry will look like. A vision is the practical expression of the mission within the context of the unique needs of the community. Answers the question: **How** do we reach our community in light of our mission?

Focus Result Areas

Focus result Areas are the 6-10 key dimensions of ministry on which the leadership must FOCUS to address the needs of the community and achieve their mission. Together, the FRAs form the vision.

Focus Result Areas	Focus Result Areas	Focus Result Areas	Focus Result Areas
Goals	Goals	Goals	Goals

Specific, concrete, and measurable goals (includes dates, times, numbers, etc.) that would need to be achieved to meet the conditions of each Focus Result Area.

- Program/Events
- Action Plans
- Budgets
- Calendar/Schedules
- Role/Positions

- Program/Events
- Action Plans
- Budgets
- Calendar/Schedules
- Role/Positions

- Program/Events
- Action Plans
- Budgets
- Calendar/Schedules
- Role/Positions

- Program/Events
- Action Plans
- Budgets
- Calendar/Schedules
- Role/Positions

Done in the context of Prayerful Intercession

Planting and Growing Fruitful, Disciple-Making Catholic Youth Ministries

Cultivation Ministries is a not-for-profit organization dedicated to developing disciple-making, Catholic youth ministries. We specialize in training both volunteer and professional youth ministers, helping parishes with the nuts and bolts of developing a self-sustaining youth ministry, and producing resources in order to support both adult and teen leaders. We use an agricultural metaphor to describe the process for growing a fruit-bearing youth ministry– prepare the soil, sow, grow, and reap.

Since 1991, Cultivation Ministries has trained thousands of youth ministers in hundreds of parishes internationally. Our mission is:

> *To cultivate team-based, comprehensive, and intergenerational disciple-making Catholic youth ministries by training, supporting, and resourcing adult and teen leaders.*

Our ministry services include:

VITAL 3.0
VITAL 3.0 is a two-year, comprehensive and strategic process for cultivating an impacting, disciple-making youth ministry. In many ways, VITAL 3.0 combines all our services, including on-

site and online training, practical consultation, and helpful resources to help parishes grow third-generation youth ministries.

Training Seminars

Training seminars can be adapted for a variety of formats, including workshop presentations and one-day seminars, or expanded into weekend experiences. Our presentations are interactive, application-oriented, and include dynamic multimedia and printed handouts.

Youth Ministry Consulting

Cultivation Ministries offers a variety of consulting and supportive services for parishes that want to start up or revitalize their existing youth ministries. Expert staff work alongside parish leaders and key stakeholders, helping parishes develop a vision, strategic plan, and structure for a disciple-making youth ministry.

Ministry Resources

Cultivation Ministries has produced helpful resources for parish youth ministers, including the books *Growing Teen Disciples* and *Positively Dangerous*. A full list of books and videos can be found at www.cultivationministries.com.

The Institute for New Youth Ministers

Designed by veteran youth ministers, the INYM is a preparation checklist and road map just for the new youth minister. The four day conference helps new youth ministers (0 to 5 years experience) focus on developing the right vision, the right lifestyle, the right relationships, and the right practical methodologies for growing a vibrant, disciple-making youth ministry.

To find out more about our services and resources, please contact us:

Cultivation Ministries

P.O. Box 662
St. Charles, IL 60174
info@cultivationministries.com
630-513-8222
www.cultivationministries.com